CHURCH
PLANTING

By Making Disciple-Makers
By Matthew Fretwell

TIMELESS
— PUBLICATIONS —

Timeless Publications Ltd.,
Castlerock,
Northern Ireland.

© Matthew Fretwell, 2020 First Published in the UK, 2020

ISBN 978-1-8381641-1-9

Endorsements

In this timely book, Matt rightly highlights the absolute necessity of putting disciple-making at the core of any attempt to plant a movement that is likely to have any serious, long-term, impact. This book is a gem, packed with insights and handy tools. To say that the church needs to recover the lost art of disciple-making as foundational activity is surely an understatement. Non-discipleship undermines all that Jesus seeks to do through the agency of his church. This alone, makes it a critical issue for church planters to factor into their primary model of church, no matter what their context. Matt does a great job of explaining why this is the case. *Church Planting by Making Disciple-Makers* deserves a good read!

ALAN HIRSCH

Founder of Forge Missional Training Network & Movement Leaders Collective Author on books on missional spirituality, leadership, and organizations.

We all know that the Church is to be about disciple-making, however, Matt Fretwell has written a masterful roadmap to guide us. This book *Church Planting by Making Disciple-Makers* clearly leads us to see this will only happen as we are motivated by the love of God, empowered and led by the Spirit of God, and serving to the glory of God. This book is transformational.

JOHNNY HUNT
Senior Vice President of Evangelism & Leadership
North American Mission Board

Love this book, especially the concept of "withness." We long ago turned disciple-making into something it's not. It's not head-knowledge; it's heart-knowledge stemming from relationships centered on Jesus. We've over-complicated the simple into the unworkable. Matthew Fretwell gets it and offers a pathway back to reality. As he writes, church multiplication seems quite the natural outfall of withness. As our country totters, we need this book as an antidote to our poison.

RALPH MOORE
Founder Hope Chapel Churches
Church Multiplication Catalyst for Exponential.org

The emphasis on church planting among evangelicals over the past few decades has been necessary and welcomed. However, many of the resources related to the topic emphasize strategies and approaches that fail to follow the biblical design of making reproducing disciple makers as Jesus commissioned his followers to do. In this timely book, Matt Fretwell makes the significant connection between making reproducing disciples and church planting strategy. I'm thrilled about his contribution to the conversation because he not only writes about the connection, but he also lives it out. I've known and interacted with Fretwell for the past seven years and I've observed his commitment to live out what he's writing about. Clear, concise, and focused on the one competency at the heart of the Great Commission, *Church Planting by Making Disciple-Makers* shouldn›t just be on your bookshelf; it should be on that short list of books that you draw from on a regular basis.

GEORGE G. ROBINSON

Associate Professor of Evangelism and Missions
Bailey Smith Chair of Evangelism
Southeastern Seminary, Wake Forest, North Carolina

Much contemporary church planting in the United States is about shuffling the sheep throughout the Kingdom. At the end of the day, we have more churches but not more disciples. Fretwell challenges this paradigm by returning to the Scriptures to provide church planters with a simple, practical, and adaptable strategy. He calls attention to disciple-making from the harvest fields. Even if you do not completely agree with what is found within these pages, you will be challenged to consider why you do what you do when it comes to the Great Commission. Here is a helpful guide birthed from the author's experience in the trenches. No ivory tower here!

J. D. PAYNE
Professor of Christian Ministry
Samford University
Author of *Apostolic Church Planting*

Matthew is both an academic and a practitioner. That is a hard combination to find in regard to disciple making practices. He has shaped young disciples, teams, organizations and denominations in these principles and will continue to shape many more. He is a wealth of wisdom!

Alan Briggs
Leadership Coach and Author

Too often, church planters focus on nuts and bolts at the expense of discipleship. We need to get back to the original disciple making mandate of Jesus Christ as the foundation for why we plant new churches. I am happy to commend to you, *Church Planting by Making Disciple-Makers*. May it spark a fresh disciple making movement through church planting!

REV. DR. WINFIELD BEVINS
Director of Church Planting
Asbury Seminary
Author of *Marks of a Movement*

Most people plant churches the wrong way. Matt Fretwell is passionate about making disciples who make disciples. This book lays out the process and strategies of reproducible disciple making that is essential to planting churches.

PEYTON JONES
Author of *Church Plantology, Reaching the Unreached,* and *Church Zero*

Church Planting by Making Disciple-Makers is an important book for our time. I have been involved in church planting efforts in South America and Southeast Asia for over sixteen years. The most successful church planting efforts I have been part of are the ones that grasp the principles communicated in this book. I have helped implement much of what I have learned overseas into a church planting effort in Virginia that is focused on reaching the "dones" and re-engaging them in disciple making. This book will be a valuable resource in those efforts.

PATRICK HUBBARD II
Founder and President
Living Bread Ministries

Church Planting by Making Disciple-Makers will be one of my "must-read" books for every church planter I meet or coach. It is that rare blend of the biblical, analytical, practical, spiritual, and personal. In our rapidly changing culture, these pages contain the timeless principles from Jesus that will empower the church to adapt, thrive and multiply.

LARRY WALKEMEYER, D. MIN.
Lead Pastor, Light and Life
Director of Equipping & Spiritual Engagement, Exponential
Trustee, Azusa Pacific University

We are in a crisis moment today in regard to church planting in the US. Somewhere along the way, the notion of church planting as an outcome of the Great Commissions has turned into an expression of marketing hype, flexing on social media, business savvy, and entertainment techniques. For most, church planting is synonymous with launching worship services that cater to the tastes and consumer behaviors of Christians. We've missed something key ... in *Church Planting by Making Disciple-Makers* Matt Fretwell brings us back to the core of the Great Commission—that we're to go throughout the world making followers of Jesus (a.k.a disciples). When people respond to the gospel and begin learning about the way of Jesus a church is born. But it is more than that. As Matt explains, Jesus' goal was to make *disciple-makers,* thus multiplication. Let this book guide you back to this basic truth that we've somehow lost."

DR. SEAN BENESH

Author of *Intrepid: Navigating the Intersection of Church Planting + Social Entrepreneurship*

Having walked with Matt over the last few years through school, life, and church planting, I can assure you that this book contains the understanding that drives him to passionately pursue the mission of God through reproducing disciple-makers. I've personally watched Matt practice all that he recommends to you as a ministry practitioner. In these pages, he will take you on a journey of understanding the current realties and needs of the church in relation to disciple making, make a compelling case for why the church must be intentionally active in multiplying disciples and disciple-makers, and suggest a framework for multiplying disciples and disciple-makers for you to apply in your ministry setting. Apparently, Matt is also a future Little League Hall of Famer. It's quite a story! To learn more about that story and what that has to do with your desire to be active in God's mission through disciple-making (and believe me – it does!), be sure to pour through the pages of this book with an open mind , eager to learn how you can be used of God to expand His Kingdom through reproducing disciple-makers.

DR. MARK CUSTALOW,
Regional Catalyst with SBC of Virginia,
Founder/Executive Director of First Nations Gospel Storyers

Dr. Matt Fretwell is one of the top experts in the area of Church planting and discipleship! He is not only a scholar, but a true practitioner, as he has successfully planted several churches. He has a heart for the lost, unchurched, and those who need true community. It also is a pleasure serving with him at Regent University, School of Divinity, where he teaches Church Planting, training up the next generation of church planters who will be real disciple-makers! I highly recommend this excellent book. It will stretch you, challenge you, and help you become a successful disciple-maker as a church planter!

DANIEL B. GILBERT, PH.D.

Director of the Masters' Program and Assistant Professor
Regent University, School of Divinity
Founder & President of EmPowered Living International Ministries
Author, *The Big 5: Discovering the Five Foundations Every Christian Should Know*
Dedicated to the *Missio Dei Trinitatis* and *Missio Ecclesiae*.

Contents

Introduction

We've all heard the statistics—Western Christianity is severely declining. This isn't Henny Penny, or the sky is falling, but a reality. With 80 to 85 percent of churches in America either plateauing or in decline, an urgent plea for reproducible discipleship and multiplicative church planting exists.[1] We know that to merely sustain the current pace of population growth, American churches would need to plant at least 2,900 new churches every year, with some estimates weighing in closer to 15,000.[2]

We don't need to go too far back into American history to notice that a transformation has occurred. Just one hundred years ago, back to the 1920's, Christianity was once so enmeshed within its culture that capitalism and faith were nearly inseparable—it was virtually improbable to receive a bank loan without church embership.[3] John D.

1   Aubrey Malphurs, *Look Before You Lead: How to Discern and Shape Your Church Culture* (Grand Rapids: Baker Books, 2013), 200.

2   David T. Olson, *The American Church in Crisis: Groundbreaking Research Based on a National Database of Over 200,000 Churches* (Grand Rapids: Zondervan, 2008), 181.

3   Charles Edward Harvey. 1982. "John D Rockefeller, Jr and the Interchurch World Movement of 1919-1920: a different angle of the ecumenical movement." *Church History* 51, no. 2: 203. *ATLA Religion Database with ATLASerials*, EBSCO*host* (accessed July 7, 2015).

Rockefeller, who organized the Interchurch World Mission (IWM), once proclaimed: "A Christian is a Christian no matter what church he belongs to...What nobler aim can a man have in life than to be Christ-like?"[4]

Studying Rockefeller's business practices, it would not be against popular opinion to question his biblical faith, but like many Americans, Rockefeller assumed that everyone in American society was automatically Christian. Alan Hirsch clarifies this by saying: "In the American expression, Christianity was not married to the state, but is nonetheless seen to be an inextricable part of American culture and identity; until the last thirty years or so, if you were American, you were a Christian."[5] This means that church membership was more about being a part of the social norms and values than it was conviction of the heart.

An interesting statistic from the North American Mission Board (NAMB) shows research concerning American churches. NAMB found that in 1900 there were twenty-eight churches for every ten thousand people; by 1950 that number declined to seventeen; by the year 2000 it declined even more to twelve; and by 2004, it was down to eleven![6] There are no current numbers, at least that I have discovered.

David Olson's statistics displayed that only 17.5% of the population in North America was attending Sunday

---

4   Ibid., 200.

5   Alan Hirsch, and Dave Ferguson, *On the Verge: A Journey into the Apostolic Future of the Church* (Grand Rapids: Zondervan, 2011), 130.

6   Ed Stetzer, *Planting Missional Churches* (Nashville: Broadman & Holman Publishers, 2006), 9.

services,[7] but Doug Murren of the Murren Group declared that number to be too high and suggested Olson's 2008 numbers were lagging a bit behind—his ghastly number of only 12% is staggering.[8] Furthermore, Murren's research indicated that "20% of people leave their church every year, which would require a visitor rate of at least 30% of a church's size per year, *just to grow*."[9]

The Western church is surely in decline and hemorrhaging as the culture pulls away from Christianity. The Barna Group assesses that "more than one-third of America's adults are essentially secular in belief and practice."[10] With a population of roughly two hundred forty million Americans, one hundred seventy million of them (71%) either consider themselves as having no religious affiliation at all or Christian in name only.[11] As J. R. Woodward observed: "Functional Christendom has given way to a 'spiritual,' secular and pluralist society where a growing number view the church with suspicion and

---

7   David T. Olson, *The American Church in Crisis: Groundbreaking Research Based on a National Database of Over 200,000 Churches* (Grand Rapids: Zondervan, 2008), 181.

8   Doug Murren, "De-Churching or Re-Gathering," themurrengroup.com, March, 2015, accessed March 2, 2015, http://www.themurrengroup.com/de-gathering-or-re-gathering.html.

9   Ibid., 5.

10   George Barna, and David Kinnaman, *Churchless: Understanding Today's Unchurched and How to Connect with Them* (Carol Stream: Tyndale House Publishers, 2014), 16.

11   Aubrey Malphurs, *Planting Growing Churches For the 21ʳᵗ Century: A Comprehensive Guide for New Churches and Those Desiring Renewal*, 3ʳᵈEd. (Grand Rapids: Baker Books, 2004), 12.

some with downright disdain."[12] **The Western world has officially become a mission field and is in dire need of an apostolic movement.**

However, while it's good to recognize numbers and statistics, the church should not become depressed—only motivated. As the culture shifts, the contemporary church must be reminded that it's not in the first century; although I believe the twenty-first century is mirroring the first in many ways. As early church historian Michael Green notes, "They lived in a world more relativist and far more pluralist that our own."[13] Of course, to some, like Ted Turnau, who projects in his book, *Popologetics*, that "each idolatrous cultural act inspires another that is darker and more deceptive," this would place humanity into a more corrupt culture than ever before, if that is possible.[14]

It's probably safe to say that humanity is, well, humanity, and a depraved unregenerate people will not flock to the gospel, but toward sinful tendencies. One cannot fault culture for shifting, or humanity for embracing relativism, new age spiritualism, or even atheism. If the church is not spreading the love of the gospel and making disciples within its community, then the current culture cannot be faulted for failing to possess a Christian worldview. David Hesslegrave defines by saying: "A worldview is formed by

---

12   J.R. Woodward, *Creating a Missional Culture: Equipping the Church for the Sake of the World* (Downers Grove: IVP Books, 2012), 30.

13   Michael Green, *Evangelism in the Early Church*. Rev. ed. (Grand Rapids: Wm. B. Eerdmans, 2004), 21.

14   Ted Turnau, *Popologetics: Popular Culture in Christian Perspective* (Phillipsburg: P & R Publishing, 2012), 65.

hearing and learning a big story with a beginning, a middle, and an end."[15]

The church is failing to present a transformation story in Christ, filled with the Scriptures, and the application from within our current lives. Society is only doing what is expected of it, to live life according to the desires of the heart. Western culture must be one of our mission fields, engaged by a missional people with a passionate and harmonious unified church at its core. **The present culture has shifted from the church to the workplace—hence, the church must engage the marketplace—and engage it as a movement.**

The call for an apostolic movement is vital. If, as Malphurs states, "Only five to twenty-five percent of pastors are equipped to turn around churches," then only a paradigm shift in thinking will work.[16] J. D. Payne rightly observes that the American church, which once was filled with missional church planters, has developed into a pastoral missiology of "maintenance and conservation of structures and organizations."[17] Hirsch adds to this line of thinking, "We forgot that it's not so much that the church has a mission as that the mission has a church…missional church is apostolic church."[18] **To combat the decline of Western culture, the church must reengage in its apostolic church**

15 David J. Hesselgrave, *Planting Churches Cross-Culturally: North America and Beyond* (Grand Rapids: Baker Academic, 2008), 146.

16 Malphurs, *Look Before You Lead,* 173.

17 J.D. Payne, *Pressure Points: Twelve Global Issues Shaping the Face of the Church* (Nashville: Thomas Nelson, 2013), 24-25.

18 Hirsch and Ferguson, *On the Verge,* 130-132.

planting past, while communally embracing its missional disciple-making future.

Biblical and Theological Reflection on the Western Church

As Lesslie Newbigin so eloquently, yet blatantly put it, "The Christ who said, 'Come unto me and I will give you rest,' also said to those same disciples, 'As the Father has sent me so I send you,' and showed them the scars of his battle with the rulers of the world" (John 20:20-1).[19] John's passage reveals the Greatest Commission; the *missio Dei*, its theologically steeped foundation within the Omnibenevolence of God.[20]

To know God is to love him. Jesus commanded his disciples that they must love their neighbors as they love themselves; this is the second greatest commandment (Matt. 22:39). When questioned as to who was their neighbor (Luke 10:29), Jesus responded with a story pertaining to the Jews' detested race of people, the Samaritans (Luke 10:30-35). In reality, we're all the Samaritan—far away from God (Eph. 2:13).

In connection, the story of the Good Samaritan is an applicable imperative to know and love those within our culture. Christ's incarnation provides an example of not only understanding culture, but also of how God

---

19   Lesslie Newbigin, *Foolishness to the Greeks: The Gospel and Western Culture* (Grand Rapids, MI: Wm. B. Eerdmans Publishing Co., 1988), 124.

20   Ross Hastings, *Missional God, Missional Church: Hope for Re-Evangelizing the West* (Westmont, IL: IVP Academic, 2012), 19.

tabernacled within it (John 1:14). In Kevin Vanhoozer's book, *Everyday Theology*, he explains, "Cultural literacy—[is] the ability to understand the patterns and products of everyday life—[it] is thus an integral aspect of obeying the law of love."[21] **To effectively engage Western culture, the church must not abandon the ancient faith by striving to embrace secular values to become relevant, but it must adhere, apply, and act within Trinitarian *koinonia*.**

At the heart of the reconciliation of all things, whether Western culture or otherwise, is the love of the Father, explicitly sending the suffering Son to vicariously be victorious over sin and death for humanity, "through the eternal Spirit" (Heb. 9:14). The love of God cannot be disseminated apart from the three persons of the Trinity, nor divorced from the *missio Dei*, as the conceptual understanding of *homoousis* underlies the Christ as the same eternal substance with the Father; so, too, Christ is the head of the church.

Robert Webber's book, *Ancient-Future Faith: Rethinking Evangelicalism for a Postmodern World* expresses the church's role and functions within a changing culture, "Our calling is not to reinvent the Christian faith, but, in keeping with the past, to carry forward what the church has affirmed from its beginning."[22] The church was given a mandate to make disciples while going about life (Matt 28:19), through the worship of the Father (Matt. 4:10; John

---

21 Kevin J. Vanhoozer, Charles A. Anderson, and Michael J. Sleasman, eds. *Everyday Theology: How to Read Cultural Texts and Interpret Trends* (Grand Rapids, MI: Baker Academic, 2007), 19.

22 Robert Webber, *Ancient-Future Faith: Rethinking Evangelicalism for a Postmodern World* (Grand Rapids: Baker Academic, 1999), 17.

4:23), obedience and submission to Christ (John 14:15), and by intentionally heeding the Holy Spirit's voice (John 14:26; Acts 1:8). Disciple-making is a command of love.

Making disciples means that the church expresses, reveals, and manifests to any culture the reality of the Trinity's nature through the gospel of Christ. As Adam Dodds confirmed, "Jesus cannot rightly be identified without describing the triune nature of God...Although the gospel is the gospel of Jesus Christ, this gospel begins with the Father sending the Son who is conceived by the Holy Spirit."[23] Therefore, for the church to engage the Western culture with the gospel, it is to reveal God's Omnibenevolence with the *missio Trinitas*. A call back to understanding that the Godhead propels and sustains the missional church community is at its core. Woodward validates this by saying, "since the church is the icon of the Trinity, true personhood is found in community."[24]

When the Apostle Paul was called to go to Macedonia, he first made plans to go to Asia, but as Erwin McManus explained, "The entire Trinity got involved in keeping Paul from going to the wrong place."[25] **Currently, the Western church is not listening to the Spirit and it seems to be moving in the wrong direction.** The church abides in Christ, having its resolve to fulfill the *missio Dei*, as the *Imago Dei*.

---

23   Adam Dodds. "Newbigin's Trinitarian missiology: the doctrine of the Trinity as good news for Western culture." *International Review of Mission* 99, no. 390 (April 1, 2010): 17. *ATLA Religion Database with ATLASerials*, EBSCO*host* (accessed July 6, 2015).

24   Woodward, *Creating A Missional Culture*, 91.

25   Erwin Raphael McManus, *An Unstoppable Force Daring to Become the Church God Had in Mind 2001 Publication* (Loveland: Group Pub. Inc., 2000), 77.

As Christ's body on earth, the church's missional DNA (*m*DNA) exists in Jesus as Lord.[26]

Enculturation occurs when "an existent, prevailing culture influences" a church to "imbibe its accepted norms and values."[27] By enculturation, the contemporary church has separated itself from the *imago Dei*. Rather than retaining its innate DNA (2 Cor. 5:17), Western Christianity has lost the power of the cross, the dynamic of the Holy Spirit, and the fear of Almighty God. The church's enculturation has stripped it of the convicting influence of the Holy Spirit (John 16), causing, in part, the West to become the mission field.

However, all is not lost. As Jesus stated, "I will build my church, and the gates of hell shall not prevail against it" (Matt. 16:18b). The church, from its earliest inception, faced political, religious, and even internal opposition with councils, proconsuls, governors, kings, and tribunes, but the "powers that be," hinder as they may attempt, could not and cannot cease a missional movement of God.[28] When the church relinquishes control of all earthly things to God and basks in his presence, it can expect an apostolic Trinitarian movement to occur.[29] During trials, tribulations, and opposition from society, the New Testament (NT) church

---

26 Hirsch and Ferguson, *On the Verge*, 158.

27 Hastings, *Missional God, Missional Church*, 18.

28 Steve Walton. "What Does 'Mission' in Acts Mean in Relation to the 'Powers That Be'?" *Journal of the Evangelical Theological Society* 55, no. 3 (2012): 546.

29 Grant Osborne. "Moving Forward on Our Knees: Corporate Prayer in the New Testament." *Journal of the Evangelical Theological Society* 53, no. 2 (June 2010): 259.

was in the midst of an expansion explosion, and God was on the move through His people.

The church must re-engage Western culture by relinquishing its boundaries to the *missio Trinitas*. Rolland Allen expresses this as the church's primary fear when he says, "There is always something terrifying in the feeling that we are letting loose a force which we cannot control; and when we think of spontaneous expansion in this way, instinctively we begin to be afraid."[30] As the Apostles Paul and John declared, "God gave us a spirit not of fear, but of power and love and self-control" (2 Tim.1:7) and "There is no fear in love, but perfect love casts out fear..." respectively (1 John 4:18a). Therefore, in moving ahead within the cultural divide, the church must relinquish its thoughts of controlling Christ's body. The church has all the resources, power, vision, people, and God-given authority to reach the West for Christ—may we be so emboldened to do it!

Church Planting and Disciple-Making

Now comes the "how" part. Church planting is still one of the most effective means of following the Great Commission in multiplicative disciple-making.[31] While teaching church planters about church planting techniques and strategies is important, Christ mandated his followers to make disciples, not plant churches (Matt 28:19–20). Sometimes, we confuse the two.

---

30 Roland Allen, *The Spontaneous Expansion of the Church: and the Causes That Hinder It* (Grand Rapids: Wipf & Stock Pub, 1997), 13.

31 Craig Ott and Gene Wilson, *Global Church Planting: Biblical Principles and Best Practices for Multiplication* (Grand Rapids: Baker Academic, 2011), 20.

However, disciple-making directly relates to and must be connected to church planting. Instead of viewing church planting as gathering as many new people as possible into a building, we ought to view planting as developing disciples into missional members of Christ's body (Eph. 5:23). The mandate for Great Commission obedience necessitates making disciples and whether planting churches, starting missional communities, or home groups, the focus must be on developing life-on-life Christ-centered relationships.

Most Western churches are growing by transfer growth (from church to church), which is not all bad if we're reaching and engaging the "dones" category.[32] But, Great Commission obedience should not consist solely of Christian transfer growth. According to J. D. Greear, 95 percent of church growth consists of "Christian transference from one congregation to the next."[33] That's not how Christ intended his church to grow and make disciples. Think about it, was the church at Ephesus not growing because they began to relocate to the Philippian church. Was the music better at Philippi? Was the preaching by Apollos at Corinth better? Obviously, that's not how the first century church thrived. And considering the stricter guidelines to join the early church, how did they reach so many people?

---

32 "The 'Nones' vs. the 'Dones'," Patheos: Godless in Dixie, http://www.patheos. com/blogs/godlessindixie/2015/03/27/the-nones-vs-the-dones/. "Nones" are designated as people with no religious affiliation. "Dones" are Christians once engaged and committed to the church, but have become disenchanted, departing the church, because they believe they are better off without it.

33 J. D. Greear, *Gaining by Losing: Why the Future Belongs to Churches That Send* (Grand Rapids: Zondervan, 2015), 27.

One of the dilemmas with church planting is that church planters focus upon transfer growth, not conversion growth. The planter is looking for like-minded individuals that will partake as part of the core or launch group, and in doing so, explicitly lack intentional development of new disciples. As well, seeking believers leads to another dilemma—and that's the possibility of those believers hijacking the new church plant's vision and mission that the Holy Spirit has provided. So again, think about it in this manner, new converts have no concept or understanding of what church is or how it functions.

The central imperative given to Christians by Christ is to make disciples.[34] Instead of focusing on teaching trendy techniques, logo development, website designs, and Facebook ads, church planting must focus upon the gospel and making reproducible disciple-makers. While demographics, exegeting culture, and raising funds contain important value, planters are to impact their communities through intentional disciple-making. I believe the mission of the church is not to plant churches, but to make disciples that form and develop into a corporate body, known as church.

This next sentence will be one of the most important in this book and probably the most shocking—but is not meant to be controversial. **Jesus' goal was never to make disciples**. Yes, you read that right. While Jesus was *intentionally* making disciples, his *goal* was to make disciple-makers! It is all about reproduction, as the cultural mandate asserts, "Be

---

34   C. Peter Wagner, *Strategies for Church Growth: Tools for Effective Mission and Evangelism* (Ventura: Regal Books, 1987), 50.

fruitful and multiply" (Gen. 1:28). The Great Commission parallels the cultural mandate in mission and vision.

When Jesus handed down the Great Commission—God's mission to the Church—He did so with complete confidence that He had invested time, knowledge, and experience developing His followers into reproducible disciple-makers. With passion, zeal, humility, and fearless courage, the early disciples set out to fulfill Christ's Great Commission mandate of making disciple-makers (Matt 28:18–20), which in turn, birthed into small churches. And, for the first few epochs of Christianity, disciple-making existed to multiply, not for the sake of head knowledge. The early church was intentionally determined to make reproducible disciple-makers.

However, it seems that the majority of our modern churches do not possess the same *ethos* of multiplicative reproducing—even in light of church planting. Most church planters are consumed with one plant, instead of seeking to create a movement. Furthermore, unfortunately, the North American church seems to be more concerned with church growth (models) than making reproducible disciple-makers. The geographic peoples that once sent missionaries around the world—the Western Church—have now left the back door openly revolving. We are failing to follow the Great Commission of Christ in regard to reproducible disciple-making.

With less than 20 percent of Christian adults engaging in any form of discipleship activity, it is safe to say that the church is in the midst of a disciple-making pandemic.[35] While myriads of books, conferences, and seminars address church growth models, theories, and programs, as the words of Christ explain, "You've lost your first love" (Rev 2:4). Discipleship has been reduced to programs or classes and church planting to models and resources.

Disciple-making implementation and application are still somewhat foreign to the ears of the Western church. While discipleship seems to be a buzzword, the actual illumination of what multiplication and reproducibility are is evidently lost. Having served as an executive director of church planting, a senior pastor, a revitalization pastor, an associate pastor of evangelism and discipleship, and now as a teacher, trainer, and practitioner in church planting—combined with having worked with multiple denominations, associations, and organizations, I believe the majority of believers have never been discipled, nor do they desire to partake or see any relevance of engaging in reproduction. This needs to change.

In this book, the aspects of holistic reproducible disciple-making are brought forth, not from theory, but from praxis—biblical and contemporary. With vigorous research into the state of the church—we must have a sense of urgency—the statistics and evidences don't lie. But my intention is that this book will strengthen you to share

---

35   Kinnaman, David. "New Research on the State of Discipleship." www.barna.org. December 1, 2015. Accessed January 15, 2016. https://www.barna.org/research/ leaders-pastors/research-release/new-research- state-of-discipleship#.VqDc-JFJQmDU.

Christ's reproducible ways and apply the importance of His disciple-making command.

Within the pages of this book come years of personal experience—not only within academia, but more essential—in everyday life. However, throughout the book, I utilize an acronym that I "coined" RDM (reproducible disciple-making), which must be understood. My passion and desires are to assist you in understanding how the church arrived at our current crossroads. Furthermore, as a major proponent of the APEST model, you may find it odd that I leave that aspect out of the book. That's intentional. This book is not meant to reinvent the wheel. Many of my contemporaries do a much better job at presenting the APEST model.[36]

As a guide to where this work will lead you, the first two chapters explore the discipleship troubles that abide over the modern church. I'll take the reader on a brief journey through ecclesiastical history and how discipleship evolved, answering the question, "How did we get here?" I believe this is one of the most eye-opening aspects of Evangelicalism. For the record, most of the research was carried out during my doctoral work. I mention that so that you know that it was peer-reviewed—they are not my opinions. Chapters three through six will address some of our current church models and modern evangelism in relation to disciple-making.

The remainder of the book will be about the praxis of disciple-making and church planting. If you love the

---

36 Alan Hirsch, *The Forgotten Ways: Reactivating Apostolic Movements.* (Grand Rapids: Brazos, 2016).

practical side of things, you will love those chapters, but if you skip right to them, you'll miss the reality of why things are the way they are. By the time you complete this work, I believe you will become enlightened and inspired with this collective and collaborative research, hopefully, using the knowledge in practical ways.

Church Planting by Making Disciple-Makers won't be one of those books that merely provides theology, ecclesiology, missiology, statistics, and theories—the book in your hand is also loaded with practical applications, real-life experiences from contemporary church planting, church revitalization, para-ministries, non-profits, organizations, and associations, along with life-on-life living. There are numerous citations throughout the book, not just for clarity, but for validation. In addition, the citations are a means for you to do your own research and study. Whether you're in church planting or revitalization, I pray that you will enjoy and share this applicable disciple-making resource.

Matt Fretwell

The Red Bat

I created a monster! Not as scary as Dr. Frankenstein's monstrosity—but nonetheless, a colossal monster—at least for poor Ryan. However, it didn't take an electricity freak or a rocket-scientist to read Ryan's countenance. I could see from the glazed-over look on his face that he had regretted ever saying yes. Ryan wasn't the monster—the monster was in my teammates' belief system. Let me explain.

I love the game of baseball—I always have. When I was about nine years old, I think I ate, slept, and dreamed of becoming a major league ball player. Most boys do, at least, in the America that I grew up in. I once actually slept in my uniform because I couldn't wait to play the next morning. My friends and I breathed baseball—it was truly America's past-time. There's nothing more American than baseball and apple pie.

I was one of those kids that laid out my duds on the bed the night before (if I wasn't sleeping in them)—I can see it now—that thick itchy white polyester short sleep shirt with the big red Y (YMCA) on the front, the same itchy white polyester pants, but with a really cool red stripe down the leg, and the red stirrups. Stirrups were seriously cool—they made you feel like a ballplayer. Those were the days—the 70's—every kid played baseball, even kids who weren't that good—and it was ok to not be good—at least at age nine.

However, Ryan wasn't just any kid—for a nine-year-old, his glove was like a vacuum. The penultimate first baseman! I thought he was like Chris Chambliss (I was a die-hard Yankees fan, still am—sorry haters). Anyway, I liked Ryan, he was a good kid. Ryan was also humble and quiet. But, Ryan's best attribute was his beautiful shiny aluminum red bat. It was amazing! A sight to see!

There was never a smudge or a dent on Ryan's bat, not one ding, or even a smear—he even had a towel to polish it. The best part—Ryan's bat matched our uniforms and it really made him look like a ballplayer—red and white uniforms, red hat, and red bat—that's extremely important at age nine! Regardless of how you played, it was essential to look good.

As I stated, I was always ready to play ball on the night prior to the game. So, what happened next had to be a God-moment. One sunny Spring Saturday morning, I had forgotten to bring my old chipped-and-dented-hand-me-down-wooden Louisville Slugger—I wasn't nearly as cool as Ryan. Plus, my dad was real old school, a purist (which evidently, now I have become). My dad was one of those guys that if I asked for workout equipment, he'd insist that raking leaves was an excellent shoulder-builder. If I wanted those cool plastic and metal tools used to make your forearms and grip stronger, Dad made me squeeze a tennis ball. Regardless, on this game day, I had forgotten the one piece of equipment that was required—my bat.

Some kids didn't have their own bats. But those kids would then succumb to using one of the bats in the coach's green duffle bag—you never wanted to use those. Nevertheless, while all the kids used aluminum bats, I had to use a wooden one—my dad insisted. But it never stopped me from wanting to take my cuts with Ryan's red bat! One day, I'd think, maybe he'd let me use it. And so, as the story goes, on that fate-driven Saturday, without my crusty-trusty Louisville Slugger, I begged Ryan to let me use his most prized possession.

I pleaded, "Please, Ryan, let me use your bat—I forgot mine and the ones in the equipment bag are worse than mine!"

He wasn't sold out on the idea—but, he eventually caved into my prodding. He cautiously grumbled, "Uh—well, I guess so. Don't break it."

How could I break an aluminum bat? I don't even think Bo Jackson could do that (even though this was way before everyone knew Bo). Nevertheless, there I was, like Ralphie from *A Christmas Story*, holding the equivalent to his "Red Ryder, carbine action, 200 shot, range model air rifle, with a compass in the stock and this thing that tells time."

Oh boy, the earth stopped rotating—it was spectacular! Walking to home plate had never felt so good! I was George Brett, Reggie Jackson, and Sweet Lou Pinella, all rolled into one. I dug into the batter's box, tapped home plate, but not my cleats—Ryan was staring intently. That Saturday morning, it seemed that all of the planets had aligned, and I could do no wrong. My first time at the plate—home run!

The next time up—home run! The next time making my appearance—I hit another home run, and then finished the day with a double!

I'll bet you that my third homerun ball is still rolling—that shortstop never did see it go between his legs, and the left fielder would still be staring out into space, if his coach hadn't called out to him. Needless to say, by the end of the game, it was too late—I had fed the monster a four-course meal—a belief system based off empirical evidences.

For the next several weeks, Ryan had no rest. The other teammates surrounded Ryan like the plague—everyone begged to use his red bat. Why not? Surely that red bat had magic powers—like Frosty's hat! It had an extra wham, more pizzazz, and after all, it was new—and shiny (except for the oops)!

I can laugh now and upon remembering that epoch of baseball prowess, I can see how little league baseball resembles modern discipleship. It's like the belief system that encompassed Ryan's red bat. I see the same scenario happen all the time.

Walking onto the evangelical field is a new guy with a giant church and a shiny new book. Then there's a new model and a new program that comes out of it. They're the "red bats" for pastors, planters, and church growth gurus. And, perhaps, proverbial homeruns were hit out of the park with those "models." And, so, everyone wants to apply them to their congregations and church planting efforts.

Well, I'm sorry and I hope that I don't disappoint you—this book is not about any secret, it's about going back to the basics. This book is about taking a deeper look at reproducible disciple-making and how to effectively and practically engage in it. **There is no "red bat."**

As a student of the Bible, the early church, and its movements, I've studied ecclesiastical history, trends, models, programs, curriculums, organizations, and theoretical books for years. I live for disciple-making. It's a passion of mine—mainly because I'm a people person—a tried and true extrovert (until I'm worn out and turn introvert). But, I don't think that anyone needs to be an extrovert to be a good disciple-maker. What we need is the right understanding, not another red bat.

Historical Red Bats

During the reign of King Ahaz of Judah, Syria and the northern tribes of Israel were in a pact of war. The king of Syria and the king of Israel were waging war against the southern tribe of Judah. Ahaz was not a God-follower—so, it's not surprising when he stripped the gold and silver from the Temple to use for protection money. Ahaz was in great fear. So, without seeking God, he gifted the Temple treasuries to Tiglath Pileser III, King of Assyria—historically known as a brutal dictator-warrior.

The price was paid. Tiglath Pileser accepted the money, went to battle for Judah, defeated Syria and Israel, and Ahaz was happy. The recording of this incident is in 2 Kings:

"The king of Assyria listened to him. The king of Assyria marched up against Damascus and took it, carrying its people captive to Kir, and he killed Rezin. When King

Ahaz went to Damascus to meet Tiglath-pileser king of Assyria, he saw the altar that was at Damascus. And King Ahaz sent to Uriah the priest a model of the altar, and its pattern, exact in all its details" (2 Kings 16:9–10).

Once King Ahaz took a glance at Tiglath Pileser's altar, it became an immediate "red bat" moment. Home run! Ahaz had to have an altar exactly like the King of Assyria's. Assuredly, Ahaz was thinking that the reason Tiglath Pileser was so successful in his military might was that he worshiped with the right tools.

There are many examples of this throughout human history, especially in war—whether it be in horses, chariots, spears, swords, or modern-day tanks, planes, and warships. But, spiritually speaking, humans tend to navigate an attraction horizontally instead of vertically. Our focus shifts from upward to outward.

Maybe it's just me, but I feel as if God is always wanting to do something unique and something a little bit different with me—something that will never come easy, but with grind, hard work, and intentionality—and bathed in prayer. So, I ponder the question, when things aren't working the way that we planned, shouldn't our first response be all about seeking God, instead of seeking a program? I think it should. I bet that you do, too.

What about the most widely known "red bat" story of Scripture—David and Saul's armor? At first, Saul and the others were extremely hesitant and stood in disbelief that David would be a formidable opponent to the great Philistine warrior, Goliath. But, after David convinced Saul and his men that he had fought lions and bears and that

God had always delivered his enemies into his hand, Saul decided that David should use his red bat. The Scriptures state, "Then Saul clothed David with his armor. He put a helmet of bronze on his head and clothed him with a coat of mail" (1 Sam. 17:38).

However, David didn't feel himself—Saul's armor and sword were not a good fit for him. We're informed that "David strapped [Saul's] sword over his armor. And he tried in vain to go, for he had not tested them. Then David said to Saul, 'I cannot go with these, for I have not tested them.' So, David put them off" (1 Sam. 17:39). I know the feeling that David had. Sometimes the curriculums and programs seem like a good idea because they work with other churches and other people, it seems they should work for me in the same manner. But I have a difficult time relating them to my context. Maybe if David had used Saul's armor and sword in other battles, he may have felt more comfortable? It's possible—but could it be why they wouldn't work is because they were never meant to work for him?

Yet, instead, David used what he was familiar with— he stuck with the tools that God had blessed. And so, the Scriptures state that David "took his staff in his hand and chose five smooth stones from the brook and put them in his shepherd's pouch. His sling was in his hand, and he approached the Philistine" (1 Sam. 17:40). Likewise, I think back to my own red bat incident with Ryan. The next game I used my good ole, tried and true, beat up Louisville Slugger. As a matter of fact, I stuck with wooden bats all the way through high school, while everyone else adapted to the aluminum ones. I was more comfortable with the wood. I admit that Ryan's bat was not the reason I hit three home runs. Actually, I was a good ball player; I worked hard at understanding and playing the game and I practiced, a lot!

The point here is not that all programs and curriculums are bad, to the contrary, for those who are utilizing no tools, no sling of their own, no Louisville Slugger; they need some type of "red bat." But, we should also presume that the outcomes will be different. There's nothing wrong with adapting programs to fit the context and culture. Unfortunately, too many people want to be like others instead of being the unique person/church that God desires them to be. By using someone's model, there's no Spirit vision and a lack of creativity.

Cobblers and Visionaries

When I was a chef, we used to label *cooks* who called themselves *chefs*, cobblers. We referred to them that way because cobblers fixed shoes. It was sort of an odd analogy, but most cooks seemed to lack vision. Don't get me wrong, some cooks can masterfully put culinary delights together— as long as a "recipe" exists.

In actuality, some cooks can cook with extraordinary talent—as long as there's a specific guide to follow—not to be deviated from. Anyway, we called these cooks, cobblers. Shoe cobblers put the pieces together and make a shoe—all of their parts are already present and there's no deviation from the plan. Being a cobbler, instead of a chef, was like having all the parts to a shoe. It was piecing together a diagram, but never attempting to create something from a vision. There's never an attempt to adapt from the "recipe." I should also specify the difference between a shoemaker and cobbler. A shoemaker is a designer, a cobbler is a repairer.

Anyway, I hope you get the picture. You might be asking yourself, how does this analogy fit model-driven discipleship? Imagine having a French master chef teach and train a man from Talladega, Alabama—a tried and true "redneck." I know, this is stereotypical—forgive me. Anyway, the Alabama man has learned to cook French cuisine, but he only makes masterful culinary designed appetizers and entrees. As the Alabama man steps back into his context, perhaps at a NASCAR race, he gladly prepares the culinary delights for his friends. While the food that the man creates may have been exquisitely prepared, it will not be accepted and probably not liked by the recipients. For this reason, a tailgate party is not the place for French cuisine.

Likewise, I would label some forms of discipleship as cobbler-esque—as cooking French cuisine for blue collar workers—there's no adaptability or vision—only cookie cutting. Rudimentary as it may be, the symbolic aspects of being a cobbler and those who choose to employ created discipleship programs are similar. It's the red bat analogy. It works for the inventor—therefore, it will work for me. It's odd to me how discipleship is boxed up, placed on a shelf, and sold.

During the days when Rick Warren had first written *The Purpose Driven Church*, gads of pastors began wearing floral button-down silk shirts and donned flip-flops. They ripped their churches into shocking division by insisting on Warren's model for church growth. With eyes gleaming from staring out at packed pews and lined aisles, these pastors sold out to a model instead of reproducible disciple-making. They became cobblers.

With all due respect to Rick Warren (who I hold in high regard), he stated that his book was not intended to be a cookie cutter approach, nevertheless, it became the proverbial red bat. And so, it seems that the contemporary church is more worried about being successful than getting their hands dirty. We're more concerned with butts in seats than making disciple-makers. But, we cannot take the grit and grind out of discipleship.

While I believe that there are some decent and edifying curriculums out there, many Western churches view discipleship as a Bible study or a class. And while both the study and the class are informative, necessary, and good, they lack what truly makes discipleship reproducible—intimacy, relationship, daily rhythms, adaptability, and spiritual formation.

In all of the Gospels, I never recall Jesus saying to the disciples, "Sit down together and whip out the scroll of Isaiah—we're going to exegete each word in its context and give application." Yet, in some churches, this is labeled disciple-making. Whether a Bible class or a published curriculum, the church has swerved from the communal grit and grind of spiritual transformation that was extant in living out the daily rhythms of life.

Instead of hearing the real problems that people are struggling with (grit and grind)—the one-on-one disciple-making that reproduces, we've relegated disciple-making to a class or a curriculum. Maybe those classes even have prayer requests, but there's always a timetable to complete. The facilitator's goal is to make sure that the curriculum is taught—and that's the goal.

Yet, sometimes those curriculums and classes can become info-dumps and will rarely scratch the surface of a struggling believer's life. In the midst of getting more involved with "churchyness,", we have created a monster—a collective of inch-deep Christians, biting into a four-course belief system, based off of the empirical evidences of something else, somewhere else, for someone else.

In turn, the church has become a group of cobblers blindly swinging red bats. We utilize someone's proven methods, principles, and practices in other contexts and for other people groups, expecting the same results. Unfortunately, it is rare that another church will hit a home run utilizing someone else's red bat. Why? As with David, it was never meant to be. Or as the Apostle Paul was led by the Spirit to go to Philippi, we insist on going to Asia (Acts 16:6).

However, is the contemporary church to blame? And, what about the pastors seeking to fill the pews? How did discipleship become relegated to a Bible study? What if the pew-filling, curriculum-driven pastors truly have a heart for the lost and are hoping to fill the sanctuary with converts? I perceive there's more to this dilemma. If we don't dig a little a deeper to expose the reasons behind our current model-driven obsessions, we'll never be able to rectify it.

Have no fear, I'm going to attempt to answer these questions in the next chapter regarding what went wrong and how we have progressed. Let's continue...

Disciple-Making: How Did We Get Here?

Warning! For you readers that love application and despise lengthy discourses of knowledge—this chapter may contain some weighty academic content. But as it's been said, if people can figure out how to buy a coffee at Starbucks, they can learn the principles of spiritual formation. In addition, this chapter is tantamount in understanding why we do the things that we do—why we choose red bats.

I want to start by saying, people are not dumb. We are image-bearers of the Almighty God. And the God-man, the Lord Jesus Christ, lived and "dwelt among us," teaching the disciples to become reproducible disciple-makers (John 1:14). With the Great Commission (Matt. 28:18-20), Christ commanded the church to make obedient reproducible disciple-makers. Jesus ordered them to teach people "to observe all that I have commanded you"—meaning—in the same way that He discipled them.

The "Jesus-model" is the only RDM (reproducible disciple making) to follow—it's adaptable, life-on-life through daily rhythms, intentional, inquisitive, intimate, and relational. Jesus lived out what it means to be Godly.

He showed people his raw emotion: anger, tears, contempt, joy, praise, humility, discernment, patience, trust, and love. He also gravitated toward teachable moments—stopping everything to train and disciple by example and illustration. The God of creation walked among us to manifest divine love—to demonstrate what love is, how it is lived out, and the grit and grind of addressing human sin, dysfunction, trial, and temptation.

With the humble act of baptism, Jesus fulfilled God's design and led his disciples to see how obedience embraces God's mission. Without delving too far into examining all of the teachings of Christ, it is safe to say that Christ created reproducible disciple-makers commissioning them to go to the uttermost parts of the world. But one integral aspect of his RDMs was and is the obedient act of baptism.

Within the early New Testament (NT) church, baptism unified new believers with Christ, as disciples under Christ's Lordship (Matt. 28:19–20; John 20:19–20). Throughout the book of Acts, Luke utilizes the word for baptism over twenty times in twenty-eight chapters. While we know that the book of Acts is descriptive and not necessarily prescriptive, baptism held an essential aspect to cultivating RDMs. Of course, baptism does not contain salvific properties, nor does discipleship begin with baptism—but it was the foundational ordinance within the NT church—it was a new convert's first obedient act of faith.

But, by the second century, parts of the church had developed a three-year process of catechesis prior to baptism.[37] This means, as I stated previously, discipleship began prior to baptism. However, from a NT and extra-biblical writings, baptism necessitated an examination and call for submissive discipleship. Historian Philip Schaff notes:

We should remember that during the first three centuries, and even in the age of Constantine, adult baptism was the rule, and that the actual conversion of the candidate was required as a condition before administering the sacrament (as is still the case on missionary ground).[38]

Candidates for baptism would join in the church's communal teaching, instruction, and spiritual disciplines, but not in the Lord's Supper (sacrament).[39] Disciple-making consisted of the cultivation of spiritual maturity within the ecclesiological community—meaning, the early church was making disciples in the same manner as the Twelve—living life together. Assuredly, even apart for gathering within the ecclesiological community, discipleship was the essential *ethos* of a Christ-centered life.

But just because we read the word *catechesis*, we ought not to think of a structured, class-driven, and programmatic learning style. I grew up on Long Island, NY (yes, if you're from there, you say, "on" and not "in."). Anyway, most of my friends were Roman Catholic (Irish and Italian). By the age of twelve, I noticed that those friends were taking classes

---

37 Green, *Evangelism in the Early Church*, 218.

38 Philip Schaff, and David Schley Schaff, *History of the Christian Church*, Vol 2. (Grand Rapids: C. Scribner, 1910), 255.

39 Green, 217.

called catechism. At the time I didn't understand what catechism was—maybe you don't either? Let me explain how it came to be and you'll have some insight into how discipleship has changed.

Within early Christianity, catechesis held a major aspect of the disciple-making process. While the word *katēchēo* assumed an exclusive sense of Christian instruction, within the early church, *katēchēo*, specifically related to "the instruction given before baptism, and the [person] preparing for this sacrament was called a catechumen."[40] For the early church, catechism was the participation in knowing God, His church, and its mission.

In the late first century, Clement of Rome (c. 35–99), a disciple of Paul (Phil. 4:3), provided evidence of following Christ's Great Commission by writing letters of "commands" to "instruct" catechumens.[41] Consequently, by the second century, the early church fathers, Origen (c. 184–253) and Tertullian (c. 155–240), utilized the word "catechesis" when referring to instruction and in preparation of catechumen; however, the term catechesis often "overlapped" in meaning.[42]

---

40 Gerhard Kittle, Geoffrey W. Bromiley, and Gerhard Friedrich, eds., *Theological Dictionary of the New Testament* (Grand Rapids Eerdmans, 1964), 639.

41 "Clement of Rome," Diane Severance, www.Christianity.com, http://www.christianity.com/church/church-history/timeline/1-300/clement-of-rome-11629592.html.

42 Andrew B. McGowan, *Ancient Christian Worship: Early Church Practices in Social, Historical, and Theological Perspective* (Grand Rapids, Baker, 2014), 95.

In a treatise against heresy, Tertullian equated the "catechumen" as disciplined believers in Christ.[43] And, similar to the NT church, instruction of the catechumen took place within a setting of communal gatherings and within the daily rhythms of life.[44] Without specified church buildings, the common places of RDMs were in believers' homes. The early church always viewed discipleship as a communal foundation to spiritual maturity and life—meaning, a believer did not engage in private discipleship. Catechesis was done with someone or a gathering of others.

This is what I found true about my teenage Northern friends—except, their catechism was done in a classroom—much different than what I read in the early church and based upon Roman Catholic principles and practices. The catechism that I saw did not look like early church catechism. So, what changed? How did we get here?

As time progressed, the church formed schools for catechetical discipleship. Nearing the turn of the third century, Pantaenus, a converted philosopher and highly regarded gospel-proclaimer, founded a "catechetical school" in Alexandria.[45] These catechetical schools provided more structure to discipleship than a "random outdoor meeting."[46] During the time of Pantaenus and the patristic fathers, discipleship began to be viewed as either a monastic-style of

---

43   Tertullian, "Latin Christianity: Its Founder Tertullian." in vol. 3 *Ante-Nicene Fathers*, eds. Alexander Roberts and James Donaldson (Peabody: Hendrickson, 2004), 263.

44   McGowan, *Ancient Christian Worship*, 95.

45   Green, 240.

46   Ibid., 241.

spiritual formation or a more scrutinized form of catechesis for the catechumen.[47]

The Monastics in turn, became isolated, disengaging from the world to follow moral spiritual disciplines of instruction, while the catechumen in local church settings still engaged in communal lay-discipleship.[48] We should note that a sort of "class-system" was developing that separated the clergy from the everyday believer, labeling them as "laymen" (*laikos*, Greek for common people). Regardless, the early church had a developed system in place to make disciple-makers.

By the early fourth century, the church had received an "onrush of enthusiastic converts" and with the increasing heresies and sects, a move from the *Apostolic Tradition* to a "specified three-year catechumenate" became the preferred method of discipleship.[49] As the previous generations before them, the catechumenate would partake in a three-year discipleship of communal gatherings, prayer, and instruction in the teachings of Christ, but they ended after the forty-day Lenten season, when baptism occurred.[50] The purpose of the developing catechesis was more to produce a Christian who "possessed the treasured knowledge" of the Eucharist and baptism, known as "sacramental grace."[51]

---

47 Ed Smither, "Learning from Patristic Evangelism and Discipleship," *The Contemporary Church and the Early Church* (Eugene: Wipf & Stock, 2010), 41.

48 Ibid., 41.

49 McGowan, 170.

50 Smither, *The Contemporary Church and the Early Church*, 41.

51 McGowan, 171.

Discipleship was shifting from an ongoing and continual practice of life to a completion for membership.

Many of the reasons for the change in purpose of catechesis had to do with the widespread conversions and the even greater erroneous infection of heresies. The third and fourth century fathers were becoming more and more concerned with numerous heretical instructions. Discipleship was developing into a transference of knowledge rather than relational communal living. The church began to view the instruction of doctrine as more essential than communal experiential gathering. Rightfully desiring to ward off sacrilegious teachings, the catechumenate was to engage and consume holy doctrines, theological teachings, and spiritual disciplines. At a glance, it wasn't all bad, it was meant for good, but the shift had occurred.

The first and second century catechumen, except for partaking in the Eucharist, existed as part of the whole within the teachings, gatherings, and worshipping within the ecclesiastical community which indicated an understanding of "withness" in developing spiritual disciplines.[52] However, the shift from communal discipleship toward individual discipleship correlated with producing a didactic head knowledge and devotion to the disciplines. When I initially studied this progression of discipleship, it seemed neither good, nor bad, only a product of the contextual setting. One can see why the shift took place.

---

52   McGowan,171.

Despite this, there was a definite progression from the Acts 2:42 church of 3,000 baptized converts breaking bread, learning, and living in fellowship together, that looked distinctively different than the second to third century church of converted catechumen. Once we add the rise of widespread conversion and heresies, we can get a glimpse into why discipleship began to change.

However, after the rise of the Emperor Constantine (c. 306–337) and "state religion", discipleship evolved even more didactically and less communally-led by the Holy Spirit. If we couple Constantine's "persuasion," the edict of Milan, and more converts engaging in governmental positions, with the latter assistance of Augustine of Hippo (c. 354–430), then infant baptism may become one of the true catalyzing shifts. Just as second century baptism was a "rite of entry into" the communal church, instead [it became] a distinctive article of sacramental faith.[53]

To clarify, neither Constantine nor Augustine should receive blame for the changes, but the changes should be understood more as a contextual dynamic. When I looked through this research, I was not seeking to place responsibility on what "went wrong" or how it changed, but why discipleship ended up in a classroom. The more I studied, the more I began to see change.

With that stated, the deciding factor for the paradigm shift of discipleship had occurred within the church during Constantine's reign. Progressively, converts became "born into" the church, through covenantal baptism, loosening

---

53   Ibid., 169.

the stringent baptismal ties of catechism. While adult conversion continued the journey of catechesis, a child birthed from a believer was assumed, after infant baptism, as part of the church—sealed by the covenant of the father and mother's profession of faith and oath to raise the infant as a believer. One could argue that the child could have been discipled by the parents, and that the child was *merely* considered a covenant child and not a true believer until catechesis at a later age was achieved. I'm not making an argument for or against paedobaptism, I'm only noting why and how discipleship changed.

Perhaps, then, I would assess, that due to infant baptism, from the fifth century, and continuing into the Reformation period, discipleship progressed toward individual spiritual discipline more than communal interactive relationships concerning the daily rhythms of Christian life. While catechesis still existed for new converts, the continued practice of infant baptism shifted discipleship away from the relational communal convert catechumenate to didactic spiritual disciplines, doctrines, and devotions of believers.[54] In any case, clearly the Acts church of Holy Spirit interaction and guidance, apostolic teaching, breaking of bread, fellowship, and house to house prayer was transformed (Acts 2:42, 46).

However, the most notable reformer, Martin Luther, believed that discipleship guided the believer into deeper devotions toward Christ.[55] Much like the Monastic style

---

54   Thomas R. Schreiner and Shawn Wright, eds., *Believer's Baptism: Sign of the New Covenant in Christ* (Nashville: Broadman & Holman, 2007), xviii.

55   Allan Rudy-Froese, "Learning from Luther on Christian discipleship." *Vision*

of isolationism, for Luther, discipleship referred to Christ's inner working power and "not our attempts to imitate" the deeds of Christ.[56] Discipleship was not "imitate me, as I imitate Christ" (1 Cor. 11:1). And, unlike the early church's communal gatherings for catechesis, the individual development of personal discipleship of character and devotion became customary. Nonetheless, Luther's discipleship view did not only consist of mere knowledge transference, but also a deeper commitment to spiritual devotions in personal prayer, fasting, and the Word of God. But, was Luther making disciple-makers or guided habits of curriculum to follow individually? It seems like the latter.

Another reformer, John Calvin, described discipleship not as a method or model for development, but as an automatic title of regenerated identity by grace in Christ.[57] Calvin, a paedobaptist, considered all believers disciples, but not in the same aspect of communal spiritual nourishment as that of the early church who practiced fellowship-style catechesis and breaking of the bread (Acts 2:42–46). For Calvin, baptism became the sign and ratified seal of a "professed" disciple.[58] Calvin focused more on knowledge and doctrinal transference, with believers hearing the preached Word, than on a day-to-day activity with believers.[59] Yet

(Winnipeg, Man.) 13, no. 2 (September 2012): 55–63.; Reformation period (c. 1517–1648), Martin Luther (c. 1483–1546).

56   Ibid., 57.

57   John Calvin, *Calvin's Commentaries* XVII, trans. William Pringle (Grand Rapids, MI: Baker Academic, 2005), 385.; John Calvin (c. 1509–1564).

58   Ibid., 385.

59   Thomas A. Bloomer, "Calvin and Geneva: Nation-Building Missions," biblical-worldview.com, 2008, http://www.biblicalworldview.com/Calvin_and_Gene-

Calvin believed that all Christians should carry out the commission of God within their lives.[60] So, while Calvin was missional in mindset and action, his discipleship style was based off the product of disciple-making that preceded him. Calvin, like Luther, is not to blame—again—within his respective cultural context, he pressed for believers to become spiritually mature. However, the reformer's processes were unlike that of the early church.

Moving along into the Anabaptist movement, they adhered to the believer's baptism approach and viewed discipleship differently than their paedobaptist predecessors. In the early 1500s, separating from the reformed church in Switzerland, the Anabaptists consisted of charismatic, "prophetic" manifestations, and Holy Spirit-empowered gifts.[61] The Anabaptists believed that the proclamation and preaching about Jesus Christ pertained to "the cross" and, more specifically, identified the believer with Christ's persecution and suffering.[62]

Anabaptist Christian discipleship was predicated upon one's willingness to suffer for identification with Jesus. Anabaptists believed that the paedobaptists made "sport of holy baptism" and that only believers should partake in the

---

va_Bloomer.pdf.

60   "The Cost of Discipleship," www.ligonier.org, 2017, http://www.ligonier.org/
learn/devotionals/cost-discipleship/.

61   Franklin H. Little, *The Origins of Sectarian Protestantism* (New York: Beacons,
1964), 19.

62   Leonard Verduin, *The Reformers and Their Stepchildren (Dissent and Nonconformity)* (Paris: The Baptist Standard Bearer, 2001), 261.

church ordinances.[63] Obviously, we know the Anabaptists were persecuted for differing doctrines, but within the movement a bond of unity grew, producing a zealous communal style of devotion and discipleship, dedicated to the seven ordinances of the Schleitheim Confession of 1527.[64]

The Anabaptist's understanding of possessing a suffering identity with Christ assisted in their Great Commission obedience toward discipleship. Whether the Anabaptists caused a revival of sorts or "got it right" is yet to be determined, but they did design a tightly knit community for making disciple-makers. At this point, I will shift gears to take a look at how the contemporary church seems to understand discipleship.

Contemporary Discipleship

Already looking at the historical progression of discipleship from communal, unified, and instructional gatherings into a more didactic and personal devotion approach demonstrates the varied approaches concerning discipleship in our contemporary faith. Most modern churches would not require a three-year catechesis prior to baptism. While most evangelical churches may identify more with the Anabaptists of the past regarding a believer's baptism, the dedication and devotion to discipleship do

---

63   Ibid., 216.

64   "Schleitheim Confession (Anabaptist, 1527): Brotherly Union of a Number of Children of God Concerning Seven Articles (The Schleitheim Confession)," Apostles-creed.org, 2015, http://apostles-creed.org/wp-content/uploads/2014/07/Schleitheim-Confession.pdf.

not relay the importance of the early church communal gathering-style.

The Barna Group reports that, "Only 20 percent of Christian adults are involved in some sort of discipleship activity."[65] With many Christians inactive in instructional discipleship, a necessity for participation in a gospel-centered community becomes essential. When researching ecclesiastical discipleship evolution, I found today's models different. I would like to present four contemporary views of modern disciple-making, their pros and cons, and which model best correlates with making disciple-makers as meant by Jesus.

Sunday School Discipleship

Historically, discipleship observed the gathering of believers to an applied study in the teachings of Christ. The early church's approach to communal catechesis might seem to correlate with modern Sunday school, but "we sometimes treat disciple-making [sic] like a program or a class."[66] A discrepancy between the NT church's communal catechesis discipleship model and the modern Sunday school model exists in a one day per week gathering, but not in a daily gathering (Acts 2:42–46, 5:42). As Walter Henrichsen states, "Jesus is calling for disciples, not just Sunday Christians."[67] Likewise, unlike the early church,

---

65 David Kinnaman, "New Research On the State of Discipleship," Barna Group, https://www.barna.org/research/leaders-pastors/research-release/new-re-search-state-of-discipleship#.VqDcJFJQmDU.

66 Ott and Wilson, Global Church Planting, 229.

67 Walter A. Henrichsen, Disciples Are Made, Not Born: Helping Others Grow to Maturity in Christ (Colorado Springs: David C. Cook, 1988), 72.

only 20 percent of contemporary believers engage in adult Sunday school classes.[68]

Yet, Ken Hemphill suggests that many factors reside into the reason the Sunday school model of discipleship seems ineffective: lack of evangelistic focus, no commitment, no organization and vision, lack of unified components, lack of fulfilling the Great Commission, and fear of innovation.[69] The Sunday school discipleship method may not develop disciples into quite the same the gathering as the early communal church, but there is a common factor that resides in the belief of discipleship as a transference of knowledge. Albeit, the early church understood discipleship as being much more than knowledge, but as a way of life.

It seems most modern Sunday school classes rely upon a lecture-based methodology of Bible teaching. The teacher prepares a lesson to impart knowledge instead of experiencing life events with the Sunday school participants.[70] Questions may arise during the Sunday school class, but the longer a believer remains a student, the less likelihood that a reproducing disciple develops— as the student relies on the knowledge and wisdom of the lecturer.[71] The lecturer continues to impart knowledge

---

68 Greg Ogden, *Transforming Discipleship: Making Disciples a Few at a Time* (Downers Grove: InterVarsity Press, 2003), 26.

69 Ken Hemphill, *Revitalizing the Sunday Morning Dinosaur: A Sunday School Growth Strategy for the 21st Century* (Nashville: Broadman & Holman, 1996), 19–25.

70 Ralph Moore, *Making Disciples: Developing Lifelong Followers of Jesus Christ* (Ventura: Regal, 2012), 204.

71 Jim Putman and Bobby Harrington, *Discipleshift: Five Steps to Make Disciples Who Make Disciples* (Grand Rapids: Zondervan, 2013), 26.

each week on Sunday and then dismisses the class into the congregation.

Most Sunday school models of discipleship contain a maximum of one day a week of gathering to listen to a leader, without receiving life application. Although, not monolithic, Sunday school may become merely an educational transference in biblical knowledge.[72] Over time, it seems that the believer does not become a student of discipleship, but a listener of the lecturer. Hence, the class is not about application, but how much the lecturer knows. If the class were to be taught with a revolving basis, perhaps, more applied knowledge than head-knowledge could be discovered.

Regardless, Sunday school discipleship possesses a few positive features, namely, gathering believers together, corporate prayer and Bible study, and collective interaction concerning discipleship attributes. Nevertheless, the negatives of Sunday school discipleship outweigh the positives as a view of knowledge transference instead of Jesus-praxis exists. As well, unlike the early church, an emphasis upon meeting once per week, programs and curriculum focused agendas, a lecture-styled learning, a lack of accountability, a lack of relational-life outside of the church building, and a more formal setting than a communal gathering are evidently not making disciple-makers.

---

72 Ibid., 25.

Discipleship as Programmatic Curriculum

A programmatic curriculum for discipleship consists of a facilitator leading a group of believers through a systematic process with spiritual formation as the goal. While early church catechesis relied upon instruction regarding Jesus' commands within communal gatherings, modern discipleship tends to weigh too heavily on a programmed curriculum. Bill Hull notes that curriculum-based programs intended to "graduate" a disciple in learning biblical concepts have become the "most common" model for making disciples within the "Global North."[73]

Curriculums designed to systematically guide believers through a discipleship course may convey a false sense of discipleship. While programmatic curriculums assist leaders in developing groups of believers in spiritual formation and guidance, believers not engaging in the programs may consider discipleship a *ministry* within the church, instead of a relational Christian identity.[74] For example, if a believer is not attending a "discipleship class," would that believer consider themselves to being discipled? Would the believer going through a programmatic curriculum receive a certificate of completion, as if discipleship is achieved? Would the class participant be encouraged to make other disciples with what they have been taught?

When discipleship exists in a ministry program, the believer may fail to comprehend the call to follow Jesus

---

73   Bill Hull, *The Complete Book of Discipleship: On Being and Making Followers of Christ* (Colorado Springs: NavPress, 2006), 36.

74   Ibid.

in everyday life. When Jesus states, "Follow me, ... and I will make you fishers of men" (Matt. 4:19), Jesus required a faithful journey into a deeper discipleship relationship.[75] Jesus led the disciples on mission (Mark 1:38), and sent those disciples out on mission (Matt. 10:5)—both encapsulated an interactive spiritual formation.

Jesus' disciples did not rely on a programmed curriculum, but engaged in a variety of methods for discipleship.[76] Programmatic curriculums tend to focus on a cognitive mode of discipleship.[77] Jesus discipled the Twelve more than cognitively, sometimes using ripened fields (John 4:35), children (Matt. 18:1–6), and people (John 9:1–3), as examples for real-life application-based learning. As Hull asserts, "Discipleship is not a program we launch, it is a lifestyle we embrace."[78] Curriculums can possess a place within discipleship, but they can also convey systematic programming and literature other than the Bible as the main method. The Word of God should be the primary source of curriculum for mentoring new believers (e.g. "The Apostles' teachings," Acts 2:42). Likewise, George Robinson asserts that curriculums do not substitute for interpersonal relationships within mentoring and unless the curriculum "serves to cultivate dependence upon God's Word," a higher view of the curriculum and not the storyline of Scripture may develop.[79]

---

75   Ibid., 44.

76   Putman and Harrington, *Discipleshift*, 117.

77   Bill Hull, *Conversion & Discipleship* (Grand Rapids: Zondervan, 2016), 160.

78   Ibid., 55.

79   Alvin R. Reid and George G. Robinson, *With: A Practical Guide to Informal Men-*

While studying God's Word in the discipleship process becomes essential, most of the facets associated with the curriculum-based discipleship models tend to illustrate the negative aspects of discipleship, namely, head-knowledge. Curriculum discipleship models exist as facilitator-based, systematic, structured, and programmed which considers discipleship as a ministry and not an identity. This model can, and usually does, focus on the curriculum instead of God's Word or Jesus teachings, and will always end (class for completion,), instead of becoming a lifestyle. However, curriculums offer the positive aspect of gathering believers together for spiritual formation—so they're not all bad or negative.

Small Groups

While varied models of small groups exist, the principles of gathering, studying curriculum, discussions, praying and, perhaps, partaking in meals, remain at the core of making disciple-makers. Similar to Sunday school classes, small groups bring like-minded believers together to focus on learning more about Jesus. However, since the small group exists to produce spiritual growth and unified fellowship in spiritual formation, some groups may unintentionally become closed and entered only via invitation—unlike Sunday school.[80]

Small groups also exist as D-groups, cell groups, or life groups, with a common focus of spiritual formation

---

toring and Intentional Disciple Making (Lexington: Rainer Publishing, 2016), 150.

80 Robby Gallaty, *Growing Up: How to Be a Disciple Who Makes Disciples* (Bloomington, IN: Crossbooks, 2013), 37.

consisting of eight to ten believers. A positive aspect regarding small groups consists in the group's form of support for individuals seeking prayer and fellowship.[81] Small groups normally occur through a deliberate, communal interaction with other believers, typically outside of the church building.

Maturity and devotion to individuals can exist within small group gatherings—whether closed or open groups. Small groups should engage in an "intentional plan to measure spiritual growth."[82] This aspect of small group discipleship entails an applied curriculum that facilitates biblical and spiritual growth.[83] Small groups convey a slightly intrusive aspect of life which should create a sense of accountability leading to mature discipleship. However, small groups also necessitate having an effective leader.[84]

The small group leader facilitates the prayer, curriculum, and spiritual discussion. Small groups desire to produce an applicable, spiritual growth and not mere cognitive learning.[85] Small group experiences may focus on relational discipleship, as believers visit with other believers, partake in meals, pray, and listen to each another. A deliberate appeal to gather weekly with a specified group of other believers demonstrates the essential principle for a small group.

---

81 Moore, *Making Disciples*, 204.

82 Chris Surratt, *Small Groups for the Rest of Us: How to Design Your Small-Groups System to Reach the Ages* (Nashville, TN: Thomas Nelson, 2015), 38.

83 Ibid., 52.

84 Ibid., 42.

85 Ibid., 38.

While I favor a blend of discipleship emphasizing, small groups and missional communities, some observations regarding the positives of small groups exist. Gathering for a meal, prayer, fellowship, mission, spiritual formation, Bible study, life outside the four walls of the church building, and even a form of relational accountability, all become healthy support for interactive disciple-making. However, some of the negative aspects of small groups exist in the reliance of a focused-gathering day of the week, which may focus upon a curriculum instead of a missional and reproducible disciple-making lifestyle and there is the need to maintain an effective leader or facilitator.

Missional Communities

Missional communities intersect the rhythms of the church with the rhythms of culture.[86] Lesslie Newbigin describes culture as "the sum total of ways of living built up by a human community and transmitted from one generation to another."[87] Missional community disciple-making focuses on a gospel-centered collective of Christ followers radically attempting to evangelistically live within the reality of culture.[88] Missional communities are created to develop a "culture of discipleship" while engaging in a lifestyle of mission together, with the purpose of makingdisciples who learn from each other, to make

---

86   M. Scott Boren, *Missional Small Groups: Becoming a Community That Makes a Difference in the World* (Grand Rapids: Baker Books, 2010), 28.

87   Lesslie Newbigin, *The Other Side of 1984: Questions for the Churches* (Geneva: World Council of Churches, 1983), 5.

88   Boren, *Missional Small Groups*, 48.

disciples.[89] As J. D. Greear asserts that, "Making disciples is more about intentionality than technique."[90] The everyday rhythms, or day-to-day events of life become lived out within the neighborhoods of the missional community.

Missional communities interact in relational evangelism within the practical side of life: eating meals, meeting neighbors, living and caring for each believer, and applying the biblical commands of Christ. The missional community enables believers to "fully live out Kingdom [sic] life within the neighborhoods and relational networks where they live."[91] Missional communities develop into communities of discipleship by creating and maintaining an "infrastructure" or "ecosystem" of growing God's kingdom within everyday life.[92] Much like the "with-ness" between the disciples and Jesus, relationships are cultivated by investing in the welfare of other people.[93] Believers share in life events, hardships, and meals, partaking in the fellowship of spiritual care, and neighborhood service, not as a missional event or outreach, but as a way of life.[94]

Many positive facets of the missional communities exist. The potential for gospel-centered community living,

---

89   Laurie Nichols, Scott Moreau, and Gary Corwin, eds., *Extending God's Kingdom: Church Planting Yesterday, Today, and Tomorrow* (Wheaton: Evangelism and Missions Information Service, 2011), 108.

90   Greear, J.D, *Gaining by Losing*, 137.

91   Mike Breen, *Leading Missional Communities: Rediscovering the Power of Living on Mission Together.* Pawleys Island: 3DM, 2013), 52.

92   Ibid., 56.

93   Reid and Robinson, *With*, 16.

94   Breen, *Leading Missional Communities*, 14–15.

building a disciple-making culture, and shared lives within the everyday rhythms of culture, includes the breaking of bread together, prayer, and a communal spiritual and accountability support. Missional communities have the Great Commission focus, due to their relational meeting, greeting, and sharing with neighbors within the community, and an effective relational aspect of evangelism. The downside to missional communities exists in the aspect of Western society's view of individualism and intrusiveness. Developing kingdom communities without a central building may not attract all people—or any at all!

With all of that stated, I view missional communities as a healthy addition to an established church setting. I tend to be attractional and missional; disciple-making is neither this way nor that way, but "both/and." One might use missional communities in the beginning stages of a church plant formation. Disciple-making involves both the attractional and missional aspects of church membership, necessitating the role of liturgy in corporate worship and also apprentice-style relational mentoring.

When Does Discipleship Begin?

Out of the myriads of books written about discipleship and disciple-making (of which I've read the majority) there's an eerily similar theme that proposes discipleship beginning with conversion. Of that, I am not a fan. I have always had contention with this line of thinking and believe it is blurring and distorting the disciple-making process—not to mention, creating a hindrance to the Great Commission.

If I asked one-hundred believers to define discipleship, I will probably get some different answers. However, if I were a gambling man (and I'm not), I would bet that the majority of those one-hundred people might respond with the phrase, "Disciple-making is about following Jesus." Assuredly, the goal of disciple-making is to be more like Jesus Christ and to reproduce. But, the question I want to answer is—when does our journey of discipleship begin? Is it important and does it matter? Does disciple-making begin once we enter into a church body as a member? Does it begin in new member's class? Does it begin at salvation? Baptism? Catechism? When? Why does it matter? I'm going to answer these questions in this chapter.

In the previous chapter, we examined catechism, the early church, and the shifts that occurred. Before we can address the meaning of a disciple-maker, we need to have a healthy starting point. Discipleship impacts and forms our spiritual makeup, our natural pulses and cadences of life, our natural conversations in our relationships, and the ways and means in which we interact with the world. I believe that to understand when disciple-making begins is an essential foundation to becoming reproducible because it opens our eyes to see things through the lens of Christ. So, let me begin at the beginning.

The Cultural Mandate

Relationships. Humans have relatedness and relationship because of the Creator. Humanity was created in the "image" and "likeness" of God (Gen. 1:26-28). Our relatedness and relationship ability designate humanity to be different than any other created thing. We were made for relationships. We have the reassurance of our purpose and design in being relationship-driven validated in Scripture.

The only time within the creation narrative that God mentions anything negative is in man's isolation and loneliness (Gen. 2:18). Humanity was made for relatedness and relationship, with God and with one another. The cultural mandate, "To be fruitful and multiply" (Gen. 1:18) is not merely about human reproduction, but an intimacy of relatedness and the primacy of love that is innately coded into our DNA by the Creator.

As Adam and Eve walked with the Creator in the garden, they were gaining an intimate understanding of living with God within the daily regularities of life. The proclamation "to be fruitful and multiply," known as the cultural mandate, was a commission—to fill the earth as image-bearers of God.[95] Think of this—if Adam and Eve had not committed sin, their mandate would have propelled them to expand the Garden of Eden to fill the entirety of the earth. The Garden of Eden would have possessed no boundaries. Every person, beginning at birth, would have come to know, love, worship, and serve the Creator by becoming a disciple-maker (talking about God and living for God).

As a student of God's Word, the metanarrative of Scripture is God's story—the Scriptures reveal the One True God to humanity. As Michael Goheen notes, "The gospel places us between creation and consummation, the beginning and end of cosmic history ... we find ourselves in the middle of the Bible as one story whose central thread is the missional vocation of God's people..."[96] The Old Testament and the New Testament are not divorced from one another—nor are they separated stories, but one continual story, much like a thread of comments on an Instagram post.

For this reason, I believe the cultural mandate is much like the Great Commission—a direct order given from the Creator to be "fruitful and multiply" (Gen. 1:26-28; Matt. 28:18–20). While there are some distinctions between the two, both relay a kingdom *ethos*. Like the cultural mandate, within Christ's command to make disciple-makers is the tantamount awareness of relatedness and relationship—

---

95   Wagner, Strategies for Church Growth, 111.

96   Goheen, Michael, *The Church and Its Vocation: Lesslie Newbigin's Missionary Ecclesiology* (Grand Rapids: Baker, 2018), 8–9.

with man and with God. To understand the Great Commission is to understand that each person alive today has been created in the image of God and participates within God's story. The Great Commission must compel God's redeemed to look beyond discipleship as conversion therapy, but as the very definition and story of what it means to be human. God's story is "the true story of the whole world."[97]

The Great Commission is a divine directive for those who have been saved by grace and filled with the Holy Spirit of God to "be fruitful and multiply and fill the earth" (Gen. 1:28). The church actively partakes in the Triune God, divine *koinonia*, and the cross-centered living of sharing possessions, emotions, and relationships within a cruciform community.[98] The Great Commission has direct relatedness to the cultural mandate because God, through Jesus Christ, is renewing the image-bearers of God, re-creating them (2 Cor. 5:17) and placing them back into the Adamic state of relationship (yet, not yet, sinless).

The cultural mandate is an "evangelistic mandate" and an "imperative to make disciples."[99] I know that some scholars may disagree with me, but I can't help to connect the dots within the metanarrative of God—that God created man in His image and likeness to know Him, love Him, and serve Him, and to fill the earth as His protectorates. The cultural mandate mirrors the Great Commission as Christ, God

---

97   Ibid., 23.

98   Hastings, *Missional God, Missional Church*, 216.

99   Ibid., 50, 111.

in the flesh, the reigning cosmic King, with all authority and an omnipotent presence, journeys with mankind as the disciple-makers make disciple-makers (Matt. 28:18–20). In the Garden, Jesus, the second and last Adam, lived out the mission of God, by and with obedience, something that Adam failed to do within his garden.

So, we arrive at a destination—a course in which God in Christ, by the power of the Spirit, is leading us and directing us in a sanctifying life and mission. So, we would probably agree that making disciple-makers should possess at its end goal the drive, zeal, and desire to be more holy, missional, and like Christ. Jesus was the ultimate reproducible disciple-maker. He also was the penultimate image of God (Col. 1:15). And, if we were created for him, to him, and through him (Rom. 11:36), then our lives must have intentionality in living out what he said and did (Matt. 28:19).

Jesus and the Disciples

The title of this book is *Church Planting by Making Disciple-Makers* means that we must look into how Jesus lived and how he began the disciple-making process. While each of the disciples was an Israelite, we know that one of the Twelve was "not among them" (1 John 2:19). We also know that each of these men (and women that followed Jesus) were at differing stages of faith, relationship, and applicative faith.

The Scriptures reveal that Andrew and Peter, James and John (sets of brothers) were disciples of John the Baptist (John 1:35–39). These men were already familiar with the journey of discipleship and, apparently, awaiting the coming of the Messiah (John 1:41). I presume the reason why they were part of the inner three was due to their advanced discipleship (James, John, Peter), but that's subjective. We can even assume that they were further along in their faith journey, per se, than Matthew, who was a tax collector, or Simon, a Zealot.

Matthew made a living collecting taxes for Rome—which would have established him as receiving a very good income and being a part of the elite upper class. As Eckhard Schnabel describes, "A tax collector belonged to the higher levels of society. His position presupposed not only that he was wealthy but also that he had a degree of education."[100] As well, the Hebrew word for tax-collector denotes a "collector of tolls" that "had to pay the tolls in advance" to the authorities—meaning, Matthew had substantial monetary assets.[101]

While Matthew could clearly read and write, his position as a Roman collector of tolls would not have made him very well liked within the worshipping Jewish community. It would not be jumping to a hasty conclusion to assume that Matthew wasn't currently being discipled by anyone (maybe in his youth, but not in vocation). Regardless, as soon as Jesus interacted with any of the disciples, their discipleship process began with the words, "Follow me" (Matt. 4:19, 9:9).

---

100 Eckhard J. Schnabel, *Early Christian Mission*, vol. 1 & 2, (Downers Grove, IL: InterVarsity Press, 2004), 278.

101 Ibid.

We know that none of the disciples had immediate divine revelation as to who Jesus was, yet the Scriptures make it clear that Jesus considered them His disciples. As well, even Judas Iscariot, who would betray Jesus and frequently embezzled funds—stealing from the ministry (Jn. 12:6), was also labeled as a disciple, called into the disciple-making process by Jesus. I point all of this out because if we're going to make disciple-makers as Jesus did, then it's evident that discipleship begins at relationship, not conversion.

Stages of Discipleship?

While I have a problem when a church or person solely correlates discipleship with conversion, I see a bigger problem with identifying and labeling stages of discipleship. I've come across articles and books (I won't mention them) that suggest discipleship as a process to be achieved. But a reasonable deduction would assume that if there is a beginner, then there is an expert stage. The problem with these types of models is in their metrics.

These labels beg the question, if discipleship has levels or stages of maturity, then how do we accurately measure discipleship qualitatively? What are the spiritual or natural markers of being a top-shelf disciple? How do I know if I am a mature disciple? Is there a certain point when a believer has achieved the mark of a top-level disciple-maker? Can a believer be an expert disciple if he or she has never discipled anyone? What if the believer's doctrine or orthodoxy is not systematic or throws shade on the gospel?

For example, let's look at the Apostle Peter. We know that Peter is the one that denied Christ three times. We also know that Peter was reassured by Christ by asking him three times, "Do you love me?" (John 21). And, after Pentecost, Peter is bold, renewed, and Spirit-filled. Peter was transformed into a fiery gospel-proclaimer. He's even arrested for preaching the gospel (Acts 4:1–4, 12:1–5). Would gospel proclamation be a type of measurement? Clearly, Peter would meet the criteria of a top-shelf disciple-maker. Would anyone deny that Peter was at the top stage of disciple-making? Or would he be?

I'm pretty sure that contemporary Christians would assume that Peter was a top-level discipleship guy. He walked with Jesus, talked with Jesus, slept under the same roof as Jesus, and was in Jesus' inner teaching circle. Yet, if a metric of a top-level disciple-maker is the gospel and/ or how one lives it out—what about Peter's incident in Antioch?

Paul writes to the Galatian church—a church that is struggling with antinomianism and legalism. The Apostle states that Peter was reprimanded by him and stood "condemned" (Gal 2:11). Paul censured Peter because he was expressly representing a false gospel. Peter was trying to live according to the Law yet desired to be justified by faith. Peter refused to eat with Gentiles—essentially demonstrating that the gospel only applied to those living according to Jewish law. Would Peter still be considered top stage?

How could Peter be identified as a top-level disciple-maker if he lived out the wrong gospel and "stood condemned"? Perhaps we should demote him? Maybe Peter could go down a few stages—maybe a demotion to intermediate-discipleship? Or does he go all the way back to the "come and follow me" stage?

For this reason, I think we're in error when we try to delineate discipleship into stages of maturity. I do not deny that disciple-making places us upon a journey of discipleship, but it's a way of life, not something to achieve in stages. We're all continual learners. That means that discipleship is a journey of learning that no one completes on this side of heaven. If every believer viewed disciple-making as a way of life instead of something to accomplish, I believe we may see it as Jesus lived it (i.e. the last will be first; the greatest is the least, etc.). Discipleship begins at relationship and continues, hopefully, to conversion and then onto the process of spiritual maturity.

While I'm not a promoter of labeled stages or classes of discipleship, I would confess that there should be imitative goals within discipleship (one goal: making disciple-makers). Every believer ought to strive to become more like Christ—to live according to the fruit of the Spirit (Gal. 5:22–23). Assuredly, every believer develops slower or faster than others, and some—it seems—are stuck in non-changing perpetuity—they never ever get out of elementary learning (Heb. 5:12, 6:1). Regardless, every believer is a disciple, but the discipleship process begins at relationship, not conversion.

I would contend that if every believer thought about discipleship as relationship building within the daily patterns of life, instead of something to complete or something only reserved for Christians, the objective would become reproducible disciple-making. Evangelism would rightly be a sub-category of disciple-making, and it would be natural. For this reason, I think many believers delineate between discipleship and evangelism—the two are separated and not viewed as a whole. As well, believers become intimidated with a "closing the deal" type of evangelism instead of having natural gospel conversations with the people around them. This is what we're going to explore in the next chapter—evangelism and its marriage with reproducible disciple-making.

The Best Evangelism Program Ever!

A few years ago, I was attending a pastor's meeting. I always loved these meetings—the guys are genuine, they open up, and great conversations reveal the hearts and minds of God's servants. One time, one of the pastors asserted, "Our church is about to launch the best evangelism program ever!" As he was talking, I was thinking, "Really? Ever? Like, better than the early church?" I have to admit that my mind began to wander—even though I looked like I was listening. Truthfully, I was hearing what he was saying, but I was dumbfounded. As he elaborated, all I could see in my mind was Ryan's red bat. This pastor had selected Ryan's bat and he was swinging for the fences.

I know that my pastor friend was sincere. He loved the Lord and that was evident. But his church was struggling to grow—they were pointing their fingers at him. This same church called me in to do an assessment. I had given them my review, one which it seemed the deacons did not want to acknowledge. They had some deeply seeded systemic problems—far beyond evangelism. They were an inwardly-focused church, a church that had no intentions of changing. And my friend's God-inspired vision "best evangelism program ever" was to take these older-aged introverts, house to house, banging on doors with invitations. That was the best evangelism program ever—a curriculum designed by someone else—that worked awesome for them and "will for you, too."

My friend was sucked into the hype. I didn't have the heart to tell him that it was a waste of the church's finances and would probably fail. I have to admit that I was actually happy that he was encouraged in something and was at least trying to get the people motivated—but of course, several months later, they drove him out—it was "his" fault that they were not growing. I don't blame my friend for picking up the red bat, nor ecclesiastical history for the shifts, only our own understanding of what constitutes discipleship.

Yet, I couldn't help but contemplate, why do churches (or pastors) that are struggling think they can grow by implementing more programs—or using some else's bat? That's so little league! What ever happened to growth by reproducible disciple-making? Well, we already explored what happened there—so, our question then is reflective: how can we return to biblical disciple-making?

First, when churches are struggling, it seems that they automatically think of programs, people in pews, or the pastor, as the first viable conversational piece. This is mainly because we are consumed by numbers. At pastor's conferences, I'm repeatedly asked about the size of the church I pastor, or the amount of church planters within an organization. Or how many are in my church plant? It's *always* about numbers. Allow me to let you in on a little secret. If more than 80 percent of the existing churches are less than 200, then God loves the small church. Here's another nugget to keep, the first lie of Satan to a planter or pastor is that you're not growing fast enough. I say that because I think Satan is always about confusing us and placing a metal fog to reduce clarity. The real question is how many disciple-makers am I making?

Second, I mentioned numbers because when a church body begins to grow, usually the response to feed the growth is to purchase curriculum. I should clarify, programs in and of themselves can be good—just as numbers are not "evil," neither are programs. But it seems that we're looking for red bats—looking for that cookie cutter approach to "winning." And so, to "get creative and innovative," we gravitate toward the gimmicky nicknames. Almost every "rad" church now has a "thriving" name to match their underwater basket weaving program. How about an "empower" or an "equip" program? Maybe a missional coffee collective?

Regardless, renaming your men's ministry isn't going to change the intentionality of the men in the church. The label of your outreach won't transform a people. Anytime a church separates natural evangelism from disciple-making there is no discipleship. The reason is due to the life of the believer. When a believer does not engage in the fruit-of-the-Spirit-living in daily life, they will never witness natural gospel conversations and the disciple-making process taking place. Evangelism and disciple-making must be connected as a whole within the believer's daily rhythms of life—they're not separated—they're integrated. This means that the believer will have natural conversations about faith, Jesus Christ, tribulations, suffering, joy, love, etc. as they would normally talk about the weather or an epic binge series on Netflix. They will also talk about the church they love—it's natural. Gospel transformation evokes a cruciform community of love.

Numbers and programs *can be* true *or* false—but they *cannot be* the measurement for making disciples. For instance, a church that teaches unorthodox doctrines or has inspirational preaching can have astronomical numbers; but is it healthy? And what does the word "healthy" imply? If church health is solely measured by numbers and programs, then I think we've missed the point of the gospel. As well, every church member can belong to a "discipleship" program and never engage their next-door neighbor or co-worker. If they passed away tomorrow, would their neighbor or co-worker even know about their faith?

So, while the best evangelism program ever may lead to church growth—it's most likely not making reproducible disciple-makers. And, to my pastor friend's credit, going to homes to tell people about Jesus isn't a bad strategy—as long as it involves establishing a relational walk of Christ-centered living with the individual, even if they say, "No, thanks." Yet, some churches feel the justification that more programs get more people *involved* and *engaged*, which in turn, they equate with health.

But oftentimes, the church is merely creating more busyness of life. More programs pile on more activity for the already saturated taxi mom, or more gatherings for the burned-out dad. Statistics show that people will generally donate their time to only one or two extra settings within a week—life is that busy. So, if you want people at Sunday morning, Sunday night, and Wednesday night AWANA—

guess what? Those people are taxed out and they're probably far from being molded into a disciple-maker—they're too busy to do life. In reality, we've missed the point, the programmatic church may keep our people busy, but it's never discipling the soul.

Healthy church growth is not about programs and neither should it define the church. Just like the red bat, most programs are steeped within some method that "works." Some new expert or internet blogging guru that has never been a pastor, church planter, or revitalizer—yet, he's got all the answers—usually those books are from people who've never "done it." In my opinion, the word "program" should be equated with the name "red bat."

Unfortunately, my heart breaks for the pastors who are struggling because their ego and self-esteem are being manipulated. The newest book, the newest conference, the raddest or coolest new hipster words will never bring them back to the basics—they'll be out $350 and go home with some guy's new book, only to find out rather quickly that it was a waste of money. So, we pick up new books and swing away—if we strike out, we try another one. Maybe we get lucky? We hit a single or double—hang on to that bat—it works. But sooner or later, it will find its place on the bookshelf, next to the other coach's bats.

Likewise, when we look over at other churches and see them hit a "home run," we want their bat! We want their programs! Can we say something good about programs? Sure, without them there is no direction, with them, they can help develop and teach believers in unique ways. So, are programs bad? Not necessarily, but we should always have in our mindset that programs are not a catch-all answer—they're a tool—they don't make disciple-makers. Am I anti-programs? No, and I don't want you to get the wrong idea that certain programs are not healthy or edifying. But programs are *not* reproducible disciple-makers—that was never their design.

The point I was trying to make before going down the rabbit hole of programs is that while evangelism is always good, it can never be divorced from disciple-making. The primary aspect of making disciple-makers is relationship building. Within the relationship building, natural gospel conversations occur. Within those natural gospel conversations, we should find ourselves steeped within the follow-up process of backtracking to the people we have shared our testimony and the gospel. One of the main tenets of evangelism must be follow-up, which is always immersed within disciple-making.

Disciple-Making as Purpose

Everything has a purpose (yes, I guess even mosquitoes). When a program is designed, it is designed with a goal—just like this book. But if the goal and the design do not align—the whole system is flawed. For instance, looking back on my choice of Ryan's bat, if the coach had come to me and said, "Matt, you've got Ryan's bat—we all know that's a great and successful bat—now, I want you to step up to the line of scrimmage, dig in, look the linebacker in the eye, and get a touchdown. Be the best quarterback for our team." For those who don't follow baseball—those are all football terms. The coach would have meant well, the tool was correct, but the goals were absolutely wrong. I would have the wrong plans for using the right equipment. Basically, the goal and the design (tool) must be aligned. I believe making disciple-makers has the right tools and the perfectly aligned design.

If we're honest with ourselves, we want programs so that our churches will grow—of course, but to what extent? I would hope with the goal of seeing more conversions is for reproducibility. But it seems that people feel good about attending a "healthy" or large church. I say this due to my empirical evidence as a previous restaurant owner. I used to ask my employees to park their cars around the front (street view) when business was slow. People would drive by and see the cars and come in—it always worked. People will flock to what attracts others—and so, I cannot fault a church for wanting the newest and trendiest program available. Sometimes, it does appease the leadership and bring in consumers.

But, let's say that a church employs a specific program to make disciples. They buy a popular, on sale, box-store 12-week teaching session. This happens all the time. As I wrote in the second chapter—disciple-making has shifted from communal life-on-life transformation to didactic courses—info dumps. This equates to when I wanted to hit a homerun, but my coach wanted a touchdown. The goal of many of the ready-made discipleship programs is their design is focused not in making a reproducible disciple-maker, but it should be.

Many of these programs have the right idea about the tools (i.e. Word of God, prayer, disciplines, etc.), but the design is all wrong. Many of our church's discipleship programs have little to do with creating a disciple-maker who reaches, equips, and sends—that cultivates a risk-taker, a willfully obedient and transformed image-bearer of God who is led by the Holy Spirit, to serve Christ's mission. When reproducible disciple-making becomes the goal, the design aligns with the purpose. The believer realizes that the goal is not to learn more but to live out life with others, making more. In turn, this purpose creates an infectious movement of regenerated gospel-centered people.

Movements without Programs

Rolland Allen once wrote, "There is always something terrifying in the feeling that we are letting loose a force which we cannot control; and when we think of spontaneous expansion in this way, instinctively we begin to be afraid."[102] We know that church planting movements explode through the dramatic transformations within families and people group relationships.[103] We would do ourselves a great service to note the movements of the past, with an expectation that God is still seeking the same powerful movements presently. Some of the greatest movements within history occurred without any programs.

One could argue that the Moravians of the 18th century were the single most missionally minded movement in church history. Certainly, the Moravians were known for their 100 years of covenanted prayer and their distinct

---

102 Allen, *The Spontaneous Expansion of the Church*, 13.

103 Garrison, David, *Church Planting Movements: How God is Redeeming a Lost World* (ArkeDelphia: WIGTake, 2004), 209.

world-wide missions. The Moravian missionaries' cultural contextualization became a forerunner for modern missions and are still considered some of the best "language learners" ever.[104] But, one could definitely argue that the Moravians used a formatted "program" of multiplying missionaries—regardless of their non-denominational wonder and communal way of life. But, it's the communal aspects of cruciform community that appeal to me—the risk taking and natural boldness that the gospel brings.

When looking at movements without programs within Christian history, the two biggest occurred during the first, and twentieth century (i.e. early church, and the church in China under the dictatorship of Mao Tse Tung).[105] There are key differences between the way the two movements without programs occurred and the contemporary discipleship program-driven approaches. Both the apostolic church and the Chinese Christian movement had much in common: they possessed no specified buildings (other than homes), no Bibles (other than fragmentations), no programs (other than creeds), lack of clergy-based structures, people devoted to the gospel, and they served Christ by enduring severe persecution.

We tend to draw a central conclusion that persecution was the reason for the spread of Christianity (NT church or Chinese). We may assert that the movements occurred due to the blood of the martyrs—perhaps. But, what we miss is that within these church movements we know what

---

104 "Moravian Movement." Missions Box. https://missionsbox.org/essays/moravian-movement-2/

105 Hirsch, *The Forgotten Ways*, 19.

they *didn't* have—programs. Whether they didn't have time, weren't interested, or otherwise, can be subjective. What we *know* they possessed was the gospel, intentionality, and reproducible disciple-making. As each believer told the story of the resurrected Christ, each discipled another person and the two movements became infectious because disciple-making was woven into the warp and woof of life.

Certainly, the churches within Mao Zedong's China looked much different than the first century churches from Jerusalem and Antioch. While both church movements were missional, in the sense of disciple-making, the Chinese church was not focused on continent to continent, or nation to nation missions. The early church had a Great Commission (Acts 1:8) to go beyond their communities, culture, and countries. And both were evangelistically centered, but my argument is that evangelism is always included within RDMs. As well, proper disciple-making warrants bold evangelism. However, whether the Chinese church or the early church, we tend to assume that each (house) church looked and functioned the same.

I hear people say all the time, "I wish the church could be like the early church." I know what these early church proponents are suggesting, but in actually, from the church's very inception, it was never monolithic. There was no solidified program applied to the places where new churches were planted. Basically, there was no tool kit. The church at Colossae looked much different than the church at Antioch. Assuredly, the dysfunctional Corinthian church was much different and seemed (probably) more charismatic than the churches in intellectual Rome. Each specific church body was uniquely and specifically created, through the working power of the Holy Spirit. But each church had an unmitigated intention for reproducible disciple-making within their designed communities and cultures.

One of my favorite Scriptural passages is in Paul's letter to the Romans. More than likely, this is due to my church planting hard-wiring and disciple-making passion. But it's an interesting passage. Paul is making his plea to the Roman churches for support to go to Spain (Rom. 15:24). The prior statement by Paul illustrates his confidence in their RDM work. He asserts, "But now, since *I no longer have any room for work in these regions*, and since I have longed for many years to come to you, I hope to see you in passing…" (*emphasis added*, Rom. 15:23–24a). Why would Paul say that he has no more room to church plant (Rom. 15:20, 23)? I have heard that argument, but I am convinced that Paul rightly assumes that the spread of Christianity in Rome and beyond will occur naturally by RDM. He implores the believers to do what they are supposed to do. When we begin with RDMs, church planting and movements occur and are other churches are formed.

Too often, church leaders will attend a conference and hear how some new leader had explosive church growth. Perhaps these leaders see the model unfolded before their eyes. They are enthusiastic, beaming, and frothing at the mouth to return to their congregation. The leaders leave the conference with a sense that they, too, will have the same result if they only apply the same programs. The problem isn't in the program, it's the concentric-belief and trust in the program itself. The leader has neglected the conference guru's culture and community. But the greatest movements have occurred without programs. Instead of inventing the wheel, can we return to what we know and have been commanded to do?

Our With-ness is Our Discipleship

There are certain people in my life that I am extremely grateful for meeting. Mostly, these people have been "divine appointments." I consider myself truly blessed to have met some of the most humble, gifted, and talented minds not only within modern evangelicalism, but also in the world. I've been privileged to meet numerous movie stars, sports figures, politicians, and investors. But that aside, the ones that have had the greatest impact are the ones that desired to be invested in me.

The first time I heard the word "withness" was when my doctoral chair, Dr. George Robinson (Doc Robinson), mentioned it in one of his intensive cohorts. At the time I hadn't realized how much this man would impact my life. As a disciple-making nerd, Robinson had struck my soul-chord. I fell in love with the term because I could see it. As a visionary person, the word withness took immediate form in my mind, like a vivid painting—a Picasso of cultures, peoples, values, and behaviors—all uniquely woven together. Withness was exactly what I was doing with multiple people, every day. But, for the busy doctoral student, church revitalizer, and executive director, I needed withness more that I knew.

After a weeklong stint of cohort classes, the pressures of life, my project, and church, I was feeling extremely low and burned out. Anyone who knows me can recognize immediately if I'm "with-it" or not. On the Friday of our last cohort day, I was feeling overwhelmed and completely depressed. I walked back into Doc's room feeling dejected. I was having trouble getting my thoughts together and my mind was in a serious funk. Just as the class was to resume, Doc looked at me. I thought he was staring through my soul. As genuinely as I can describe, he said, "Hey, are you alright?" Before I could think of how to hide my emotions, I blurted out, "No, no, I'm not." He stopped the class and directed me outside into the giant atrium toward two small leather couches. It was there and then that I learned that I, too, needed witness. The rest is history, but to this day, Doc will still check in on me to see how I'm doing. It's not because he's superhuman, it's because he gets it—he cares. That's witness.

To further explain, for me, witness carries the connotation of connected daily rhythms and dysfunctionality, accountability, fellowship, integrity, love, boldness, and character. A few years after completing my doctoral work, Doc teamed up with a colleague and wrote the book, *With: A Practical Guide to Informal Mentoring and Intentional Disciple-Making.*[106] Let me be honest, the impressiveness of the book it isn't it's length, academic prowess, or astute words because the book practically has none of those. The book has grit—it's about the everyday life of a believer and

---

106 Reid, Alvin, R, and George Robinson, *With: A Practical Guide to Informal Mentoring and Intentional Disciple-Making,* Lexington, KY: Rainer Publishing, 2016.

what mentorship and discipleship entail—what it looks like, practically.

Since the word and terminology appeal and apply so greatly to me, I want to expound on the withness principle. Allow me to give you two examples of how I contextually use it. First, growing up in New York seemed to entrench the term withness, even more. The term seemed almost mafioso, a family among families that never leaves you.

Years ago, there was a movie about a mob informant in the witness protection program. The movie was a comedy based upon an ex-mobster-turned-informant played by Steve Martin, so you already know it's not to be taken seriously. In one scene, Martin's character stresses to his FBI protector, "Don't worry. I'm witchu. When I say I'm witchu, I don't mean it like an expression—I'm not sayin' I know what you mean. *I mean—I'm witchu*."[107] Yes! That's it. Withness means, "I'm witchu" (with you).

Again, withness applies to my current setting, I'm planting a church among the military in the Hampton Roads of Virginia area—the largest naval base in the world. With my Navy military background, I understand the language, culture, and sometimes, the close-knit community. From time to time, the people that you serve with in the military will endure situations that have no common sense and basically, well to put in bluntly, suck. There's a saying, "Embrace the suck." You do it together. And, enduring the "suck" together produces a comradery that wouldn't and

---

107 My Blue Heaven. 17 August 1990. Warner Bros.

couldn't exist any other way—it was a withness of life. As soldiers in combat may say, "I got your six."

Withness is all of these things; it's being with you, embracing the hardships, and having another's back. Withness is not only about understanding what someone is going through, but also *actively* going through the same things with the person. It's going through their hurts, their joys, their pains, their rejections, and daily celebrations. Biblically speaking, withness is Romans 12:15, "Rejoice with those who rejoice, weep with those who weep."

Jesus and His disciples went through life together—I love that. I can't read the story of Christ at Gethsemane without feeling his lonely angst—his human need for support, brotherhood, and witness. Granted, Jesus had divine knowledge of what was about to occur and would be obedient to death. But His plea to the guys that thought they had Jesus' "six" are sobering, "Can't you guys even pray for one hour?" (Matt. 26:40, paraphrase). I don't blame the disciples—I get it, but that's the withness of life that we all long to have. It is the call at three in the morning, the invitation to help move furniture (embracing the suck), the lending of possessions, and the sharing of emotions, feelings, and Christ.

Withness is Discipleship

There is no discipleship without living life together. One of the aspects of the Church's obsession with Acts 2:42–47 is Luke's snapshot of community—one of individuals "devoted" to corporate life. I think we all yearn for relatedness and relationship. Luke paints us the picture of a sub-culture living within a culture. The early church's birthing stages, and how they effectively live out life together in witness. They were committed to the "apostles' teaching and the fellowship, to the breaking of the bread and the prayers" (Acts 2:42). But, much more than that, Luke was describing a picture of real people. Someone prepared the meals, someone, if not all, shared in prayers and needs, someone made sure the home was ready. It was epoch of love.

The withness that we all long for is the real, true, and deep fellowship to navigate through the turbulent arrays of daily life. If the Covid-19 outbreak has been a learning experience about anything, I believe it is the lostness of touch, the unfortunate rendering of living in isolation. Notably, suicides are up nearly 3000 percent in some regions. We were not meant for isolation. Whatever the good and great things of technology attempting to bring us all together, technology lacks touch; it lacks an arm around a brother or sister who is enduring hardship. People were designed for relationship—we were made to live life together.

After all of these years being involved in church planting, I can come to the conclusion that it is not church planting that I admire or love, but the building of true relationships—the grit, the grime, the togetherness. In the church that I'm currently planting, we meet in a shared space. Shared spaces consist in places of business within the community. Our particular shared space is a CrossFit gym, Pride Fitness. As I entered in on Sunday morning, the place was being painted. Due to the Covid-19 virus we were livestreaming our Sunday discussion. So, having painters in the building was not a problem. Upon entering,

I immediately heard the sound of Metallica blasting for the painters. I struck up a conversation with one of the painters. I realized that this is exactly where a church should be— amongst the part of community that has no idea who Jesus is, or the power of His amazing grace. Without traveling down another rabbit hole, I have to mention the gym owner, "Vec." Yes, I have been discipling Vec, but along the way, he also disciples me in fitness and life. We feed off of each other.

I recently heard the former Navy SEAL, Marcus Luttrell, make this comment, "We're all blades and other people are stones. Some damage us, some make us dull, and some sharpen us." Vec is a guy that sharpens me. That's what I love about disciple-making; it's reciprocal—if you're doing it right. It's much like the Apostle Paul reprimanding Peter.

Withness. Over the last several months, I have had the blessed opportunity to walk in withness with Vec because of our shared space (I'll discuss more about this later). There's always an awesome transformation that occurs when we truly invest our time in others—not in the sense of "Hey, I'll pray for you"—but in physically taking the time to listen, to share, and to allow our lives to be open books. Vec noticed that I lived my life, not in perfection, but in obedience. Obedience is not easy, it's hard. That's why withness can never be fake — people will see right through it. Withness is inviting others to your home, repeatedly. Let them see your photos, your memories, and your family. Let them see the person that God sees. Withness is more than mentoring—it is mutual growing, reflecting, and cruciform living.

Withness is discipleship because of the relationship between broken, yet redeemed people. Withness answers the hard questions and sometimes, has no answer. Sometimes, withness sits in silence. It can also demonstrate the reality of blurting out, "This stinks!" It's knowing and showing that life is hard; it's messy and fraught with challenges; but also knowing that Jesus overcame the world (John 16:33). The Acts 2 church was not filled with perfect people, but devoted redeemed people. They had "generous hearts" for one another and toward God (Acts 2:46). They were devoted to withness.

One of the biggest problems with discipleship today is caused by human pride. We use nonchalant greetings like, "How's it going?" but we really don't want to know. For some reason, we fail to believe that we're equally saved by grace. Believers are living life in fear of what other believers might think, say, or judge. If we're honest, the church fails at discipleship because we have yet to submit to Christ, as broken. And, because we have yet to fully live submitted and obedient (non-perfect) lives, we fail at disciple-making. We want others to see a better side of us—a Facebook side that only posts the good pictures. Yet, witness is not Facebook, it is all of the other content that will never make the highlight reel—but that's where discipleship happens.

Vertical Blindness

"And when [Jesus] had said these things, as [the disciples] were looking on, he was lifted up, and a cloud took him out of their sight. And while they were gazing into heaven as he went, behold, two men stood by them in white robes, and said, "Men of Galilee, why do you stand looking into heaven?" (Acts 1:9–11).

Sometimes I think this is the church's reproducibility problem—we're so vertically blinded that we cannot see horizontally. Most of the church is still gazing upward, waiting for the Lord's return. While we're supposed to anticipate an imminent return of Christ, we're not supposed to neglect His disciple-making mission. As Bob Logan expresses it, "The main point of church planting is not actually planting the church—the main point is making disciples."[108]

I believe that most of the Western church has an escapism worldview. We're afraid of living Spirit-filled lives. We want Jesus with us and for everything to be comfortable. And so, there's a focus upward—Jesus is returning, therefore, I'm getting out here. Yet, the world is lost and broken, but now that I'm saved, I want out. The church has been staring up into the sky for so long that is has vertical blindness.

Just as the early church sat gazing up into the sky, as if watching a helium balloon lifted into the atmosphere, slowly losing sight as it vanishes, so too, I believe we're guilty of neglecting the mission of disciple-making. But, vertical blindness not only relates to escapism and waiting to leave the troubles of this planet behind, it also relates to fear. I've said multiple times that I believe the one verse in all of Scripture that terrifies Christians is John 3:8, "the

---

108 Logan, Bob, *The Church Planting Journey* (2019), 63.

wind blows where it wishes, and you hear its sound, but you do not know where it comes or where it goes. So it is with everyone who is born of the Spirit."

I think that terrifies believers. To lead a Spirit-filled life means that I will be taken to my uncomfortable zone. Terry Coy expressed it in this manner, "When it comes to danger, we are irrational ... [so] to soothe our fears we create a bubble."[109] We're all seeking bubble living, a dedicated life in Christ with protection and free from danger, despair, angst, or troubles. Vertical blindness is caused by a prolonged viewing of the sun. We've been looking and waiting for Jesus to come back for so long, with our eyes fixated on the sun, that we've lost focus on broken people. They have all become blotches to us—we can't see their hurts and pains. Instead of obediently following the Great Commission to make RDMs, we instead settle for more people in the pews and becoming comfortable in our bubble.

Vertical Church Growth Won't Make Disciple-Makers

Working my way up the restaurant ladder, in one of my first jobs, I was hired at a local place as line cook. The owner specified that the last cook reporting to his shift would have to stay late and make the crepes for the next morning (off the clock!). All of the cooks would show up early—no one ever wanted to make the stacks and stacks of those thin French pancakes—it was tedious and boring!

---

109 Coy, Terry, *Facing The Change: Challenges and Opportunities for an American Missiology* (Oklahoma: Tate, 2013), 257.

Line cooks started trying to beat each other in— sometimes showing up an hour early to avoid being the crepe-maker. The owner added another rule, no one could clock in until their scheduled time, and if they arrived early, they had to begin the prep list. He had a real racket going on—off the clock prep work. Well, I hated making crepes as much as the next guy, and my fellow line cooks were beating me in every day, even forty minutes to an hour early —prepping for free! Eventually, I just stopped caring, accepted my fate as crepe-maker and foiled the owner's plan. His free labor scheme was crushed. The line cooks stopped coming in early because I was dedicated to making the crepes. I took one for the team.

Vertical church blindness can also relate to growth models. These church growth models are like crepe-making— each event or program is created within the church to solely serve its empire. It is layer upon layer of stacked programs. And while pastors may indeed be teaching and preaching some great messages to edify the church, they and the paid staff have become the crepe-makers. The church realizes that the pastor is doing the "ministry" and never become motivated to engage in RDM—they never make any impact for the kingdom. Why should they? Someone's going to make the crepes for them.

As the church looks upward at the staff, it's the same as if they were gazing upward waiting for the Divine return. Since the church is people and not a building, the consumers never spiritually mature—they never "grow." Sure, the building can "grow" bigger with additional add-ons, but the people will never naturally grow. Likewise, the people-as-church will never grow as long as their hard work is being done for them. They may have additions built on, by taking another course, enduring a class, or session, but it's all vertical blindness.

There's a reason why I love guys like Doc Robinson, Alan Hirsch, and Philip Nation —they're real people. As well, they understand the truths of Ephesians 4 and how the work of leadership is to "equip the saints for the work of the ministry" (Eph. 4:12). While Alan has probably spent more time invested in the Ephesians APEST model than most, the truth of the Scriptures is that pastors were never designed to do all of the ministry—it has always been about the people. Just as I described in the last chapter regarding withness, discipleship is performed communally and by life-on-life, not in a classroom. As Hirsch affirms, "There is no other way to develop genuine transformational movements than through the critical task of disciple-making."[110]

Disciple-making is about movement. Do not get confused. It is about reproducing others so that they can reproduce, as well (2 Tim. 2:2). The Great Commission has always been about "as you go," make disciples (Mt. 28:18–20). Vertical blindness halts horizontal growth movement. Whether a specific church has placed all of the teaching on their pastor, or they have embraced escapism, or the focus is upon more seats and larger houses of worship, vertical blindness destroys movements.

When I was younger, my buddies and I would play tricks on people. We would pretend we saw something in the air, and, without reservation, we were always able

---

110 Hirsch. *The Forgotten Ways*, 127.

to make others look. Vertical blindness is contagious and almost as deadly as enculturation.

Enculturation and Cultural Shift

"People rarely stop to think about the inherited system and pressures of enculturation in the dominant cultural context."[111] — Alan Hirsch.

I remember being asked a question once, "How do you boil a live frog?" I'm sure that you've heard this one. Though it sounded gruesome, I quickly realized that the question was given to me as a riddle. While it's really difficult to place a lively frog into boiling water, if you place the frog into a pot of tepid water, he will swim around and enjoy it. All the while you can turn up the heat, slowly cooking the poor unsuspecting amphibian—and he enjoyed it.

Within any culture there is a chasm between societal norms and the gospel, but this canyon needs to be crossed. This is where the rubber meets the road concerning the Great Commission (Matt. 28:19), the great sending of God. The church is sent out into the world to gather lost, broken, and sinful people. But somewhere along the way, the evangelical church has been compromised. Jesus declared, "For what will it profit a man if he gains the whole world and forfeits his soul?" (Matt. 16:26a). I fear, much like the frog, the church is forfeiting its soul, without even noticing it.

---

111 Hirsch, *The Forgotten Ways*, 36.

Striving for Acceptance

Enculturation—what is it? For some of you, this may be the first time you are hearing of such a term, and you may be thinking, "Please spare me the big ten-dollar words, save them for the theologians, and just spill it..." But while the word enculturation is indeed a big word, it is important because of its all-encompassing meaning and how it affects the church.

Enculturation is defined as "the process whereby an existent, prevailing culture influences an individual or community (e.g., the church) to imbibe its accepted norms and values so the individual or community is pressured to find acceptance within society of that culture."[112] In layman's terms, enculturation is when you're pressured to follow the crowd and desire to be one of them. This is also known by teenagers as extreme peer pressure. This is not to be confused with bullying, or even the emergent church movement, no, not at all. Enculturation is more similar to peer pressure because teenagers have a desire to be the *cool* kids, they don't want to be left out of the in-crowd, especially if they're ridiculed for not following.

I am going to validate this, just in case you may be asking: what's the difference between the church wanting to be relevant, or cool and hipster, compared to enculturation? Isn't that the same thing? Actually, no; it is not the same thing. Enculturation is being pressured to accept society's norms where the culture prevails by influence. This is not the same as the "when in Rome..." theory which many

---

112 Hastings, *Missional God, Missional Church*, 38.

emergent churches were attempting to do for the sake of sharing the gospel. Enculturation occurs much like the boiling of a frog—it is slow and steady.

Honestly, the church must be different, for so it is called to be. The church's historical faith is an incarnational faith; it is "the reality of God entering into human affairs."[113] The cross has always been and always will be offensive (1 Cor. 1:18). But so that we may better understand, a rudimentary analogy will be used. Let's take capitalism which sometimes is the leadership model for the American evangelical church. In capitalism, a company provides a service which is desired, and does so intentionally to be different from any other, and yet meeting a need of its culture. For the most part, this makes businesses successful when they can maintain consistency, pricing and customer service, along with demand. A business provides a service which the community desires. When a business does not follow through with providing a good product and service, it files for bankruptcy and dies.

Unfortunately, many evangelical churches believe in this model: that the church is deemed as a business organization and must provide something that society wants. Once again, they believe that the *something* is the gospel, and to help sell it to the culture, they fall prey of changing it to make it more *palatable*. And so, they may fashion sexual immorality as not applicable to holiness, accountability to be non-existent in maturity, and the gospel to be either all grace (antinomianism), or universalist (everyone gets in).

---

113 Bosch, David, J., *Transforming Mission: Paradigm Shifts in theology of Mission* (Maryknoll: Orbis, 2009), 181.

Unfortunately, again, sometimes the cross doesn't taste so good, but that's how it's supposed to be. For clarity, I'm not proposing that it's the evangelical church's music or liturgical styles that are its downfall; no, it's specifically the enculturation of the church (and, of course, the lack of RDM). The evangelical church is more than on a proverbial slippery slope—those days are behind us. The Western church has been pressured into acceptance and tolerance, and when it does not adhere to the culture, then it's labeled as intolerant. This means anything that is deviant from the societal norm, and so the church might as well file for chapter 11, right? Wrong. The church has lost its first love (Rev. 2:4)—its unyielding passion for Christ, its mission to be incarnational and the power of the gospel to reach broken people.

The Mission and Inculturation

Here we go again, another ten-dollar word—inculturation—not to be confused with enculturation. The word inculturation refers to the mission of the church with the gospel which is to evangelize a culture by embracing how a society of people communicates, much like contextualizing. Inculturation could possibly be considered the "when in Rome" theory (possibly, depending upon how you view it). But because the church has its identity and mandate in Christ, the church is Rock-solid in its fundamental core—namely, the gospel. The church seeks the lostness of all cultures and societies by telling them about Jesus in a way that doesn't change the gospel, but helps them to understand its depth, richness, and truth. When the cross stops pointing out the sin of humanity, then the cross is no longer about redemption and reconciliation.

Let's briefly look at the Great Commission in Acts 1:8. Jesus proclaimed, "But you will receive power when the Holy Spirit has come upon you, and you will be my witnesses in Jerusalem and in all Judea and Samaria, and to the end of the earth." Why would Jesus give power to the church? Is it to conform to the world or to reach it? Is it possible that Jesus knew the cultural and societal divides in which the church was about to face? Assuredly it is. I believe Jesus knew the forces of evil, human sin and rebellion, coupled with the pressures of cultures and societies. For this reason, He gave the church authority and power to stand strong and be authentic, in Him. The church has the power to inculturate the community by incarnational living.

Authentic doesn't necessarily mean different, but the Spirit of God must move within the church in such a way for the community outside of the church to notice individual and corporate transformation. An authentic Christ-life sets aside all pride for humility to serve and be a witness to the community. Authentic faith is knowing that "God has equipped us to encourage others."[114] This Spirit-filled power for encouragement isn't merely about being altruistic, but also about being incarnational. The boldness that God has equipped every believer with is enough to influence each believer's immediate circle and beyond. With that said, God has also created us as image-bearers. We are intelligent by design.

---

114 Balzer, Tracy, *Thin Places: An Evangelical Journey into Celtic Christianity* (Abilene: Leafwood, 2007), 59.

To effectively inculturate our communities, we may need to employ our God-given intellect to think as others think. There are times when the church needs to reach across its society by using application to be able to communicate the gospel in such a way as to allow the Holy Spirit to work in the hearts and minds of people—to be on mission *with* God. For example, the Apostle Paul utilized some of the writings of Greek poets in his contextualization of the gospel to those in Athens (Acts 17:22-31). Today, we might utilize movies, TV shows, books, or social media. As I've heard Tim Keller say before, I can't recall where, but he expressed the idea that we all should view life through two sets of glasses. Everything we watch and view should be viewed through the normal face value and also viewed through the lens of Christ. This means as I'm watching a movie, I'm ultimately relating it to my Christian worldview and how to utilize it as a tool for the gospel.

Inculturation is how the church fulfills the mission of God among different people groups. However, in none of these circumstances does the gospel *ever* change, or the *identity* of the church. This is now at the core of what I believe is causing the evangelical church to lose its soul.

The Loss of the Church's Identity

It is no secret that Christians believe that God created Adam in the image of God (Gen. 1:26). In so doing, God gave Adam dominion and rule over the Garden; God commanded Adam to subdue the earth and be fruitful (Gen. 1:28), to begin and spread a kingdom on earth. To make a long story short, then the fall of humanity into sin occurred (Gen. 3:1–7). However, and praise be to God, the Word of God became flesh to redeem and reconciled humanity.

Jesus, the second Adam (1 Cor. 15:45), being crucified for the forgiveness of sins (Eph. 1:7; Col. 1:14), rose from the dead, was given all authority, and then gave that authority to the church (Matt. 28:18-19). The church exists, only in Christ, and has its purpose of fulfilling the mission of God, as the image of God. As Christ's body on earth, the church's identity is solely wrapped up and exists in Him. However, by enculturation, the church is separating itself from its reconciled state, perhaps, unknowingly. Rather than possessing Christ's DNA (2 Cor. 5:17), some believers within Christianity are more worried of being liked, than to be like Christ (Eph. 5:1). If in Adam all have sinned (1 Cor. 15:22) and all have fallen short of the glory of God (Rom. 3:23), then in Christ, all of humanity must be reconciled and redeemed. But this is not possible when the church loses its soul and gains the world. As Mike Bonem states, "Leaders need to be deeply aware of the existing culture ... but they also need to know that changing a culture is the hardest and slowest kind of organizational change."[115] Basically, if the church is not cognizant of the differences between the culture of the world and the DNA of Christ, the church will become enculturated and have a tremendous and long battle to return to orthodoxy, if possible.

I have long thought about whether living in Western society compared to third world countries is a blessing. Upon serving in Liberia, Africa, I found an inextricable and beautiful church—one undeterred from Satanic attacks, persecution, and without the smoke and mirrors. I have come to the conclusion that the Western church is the frog in the pot, slowly being desensitized and accepting of unholy, ungodly, and unmentionable behaviors. Don't misconstrue what I'm trying to say, I'm not seeking a holier than thou living, but I am seeking a holy one imbibed with empathy, love, power, zeal, obedience, and Spirit-guidance. There must be demarcation lines for the church, no matter the cost.

And so, I believe that by enculturation the church is losing its soul which has a catastrophic domino effect—the loss of identity. This causes the loss of the power of the cross, the power of the Holy Spirit, and the power from Christ. There is no longer any convicting influence from the Holy Spirit (John 16). I have told my daughters, if you are

---

115 Bonem, Mike, *In Pursuit of Great and Godly leadership: Tapping the Wisdom of the World for the Kingdom of God* (San Francisco: Jossey-Bass, 2012), 178.

ever at a point when you do not feel the convicting power of the Holy Spirit—you ought to be extremely terrified.

When the church is enculturated, it becomes a mere extension of society, a feel-good gathering place of niceties, a country club. The church loses the prophetic authority to confront personal sin. But more importantly, the church loses the power from Christ, which heals all brokenness, serves the poor, loves with compassion, and rescues the rebellious. While the enculturated church may be able to perform some of these duties—they're only accomplished in self-pride.

With that understanding, the gospel cannot be good news because there's never any bad news (human sin). A church devoid of Christ's identity is without Christ, therefore, it's just an organization, a gathering of people negated of the redemptive power and love of Christ. Love is not love if there is no discipline.

Enculturation is killing the evangelical church. It's backstroking in the tepid water, enjoying itself and oblivious to its own demise. These things should break our hearts, cause us to repent, and cling to the efficacious work and grace of Christ. The beauty of the cross is in the purity of Jesus who was slain and suffered—to reconcile and redeem humanity from the wrath of God against sin, and, for the illumination that the church has been robed in Christ's righteousness, as His bride (Rev. 21:2). The church has only one sole identity, Jesus Christ—the very image and incarnation of God. Let us not be like the world but reach the world. Let us not love the things of the world, but the people within it.

Again, let's revisit the words of Jesus, "For what will it profit a man if he gains the whole world and forfeits his soul?" (Matt. 16:26a). These words of Christ were not meant to be a suggestive warning or some type of symbolic format for how Christians view life, but a reality as to the impact of culture and society. Unfortunately, it seems the ears of the church have become anesthetized. Even the pop-culture Christian rapper, Toby Mac, made this verse into a catchy tune. It's become bumper sticker material, refrigerator Christianese, and anecdotal regurgitation. But it's also becoming a realism of the church. Enculturation is how the church is losing its identity and soul.

I believe it is imperative that the Western church re-engages in reproducible disciple-making to unleash the cure. But this should not be as some programmed curriculum or quick fix. I believe it will occur through repentance, a contrite turning back to God and yielding to the Spirit of God. I believe that through revitalization and church planting, both via RDM, the church can once again engage in its Spirit-filled nature. We must be risk-takers. We must be willing to be guided to the uncomfortable and difficult places. We must set aside our own goals of success for God's will and plan. For if we do not, as Bonem suggests, "The Spirit of God will trump man's logic and man's planning."[116]

If we do not serve the mission of God, we are not serving God, but serving self. We create our own Tower of Babel, believing that we can make our own way to heaven. That's not church planting or the church. Church planting

---

116 Bonem, *In Pursuit of Great and Godly Leadership*, 120.

is not about entrepreneurship or empire building, it is about multiplication. To be even clearer, church planting is about reproducing disciple-makers that make disciple-makers who form powerful collective-gatherings of Christ with the purpose of impacting and transforming communities by gospel living. However, as clear as Jesus could make it, He declared the salvation was a gift, but discipleship would cost us everything we have (Luke 14:25–35). Some of us know this cost more than others.

Bi-Vocational Ministry

In this chapter, I wanted to explore where I see that the contemporary and future church is headed and the correlation of bi-vocational ministry. Bi-vocational relates to the need to work in more than one vocation to support oneself/family. Most church planters and missionaries work two vocations—one as a pastor or missionary (with little to no income) and the other within the world (for a main income)—thereby—becoming bi-vocational.

Understanding what we know about the current church dynamics and the hemorrhaging of the Western Christian church (*See Introduction*), it is no surprise that the church cannot continue with the status quo. While I have presented RDMs as the necessary means for church planting, I have used these same principles and concepts in church revitalization (*See REAPSOW*). There must be an illumination within the church that the idea of "if you build it, they will come," is no longer true.[117] Western society does not believe it needs nor desires the church.

Our culture has shifted away from the church and toward the marketplace—which is not all bad. But, the

---

117 Costner, Kevin, et al. *Field of dreams*. Universal City, CA: Universal, 1999.

church must prepare itself by entering back into the marketplace, utilizing Luke's record of the Apostle Paul's church planting endeavors, and Paul's epistles as experiential evidences. While I have an affinity with pastoral care and the pastor-congregation relationship, I believe men, like Alan Hirsch, have effectively written on the subject, as well as why that our current paradigm must change, so I will not revisit what was so eloquently written.[118] Needless to say, if the church is to focus on conversion growth, RDMs, and movements, then we need a better strategy, but maybe not a new one.

In this chapter, I've included a picture of how I have planted and trained some denominations and planters to practically engage in church planting. The diagram begins with bi-vocational working because I believe it is the best way to engage the people of the community which it is trying to reach. Without a pulse on the unregenerate community, the planter or revitalizer will have a difficult time going forward. By this, I strictly mean creating reproducible disciple-makers.

Students of the Bible know that the Apostle Paul was truly a tent maker — that was his occupation and main income source. While proclaiming the gospel in missional church planting, Paul worked among "pagans in his tent-making business."[119] I think this is what I love so much about Paul, he worked, lived, and boldly preached among

---

118 Hirsch, *The Forgotten Ways*.

119 N.T. Wright, and Michael F. Bird, *The New Testament in Its World: An Introduction to the History, Literature, and Theology of the First Christians* (Grand Rapids: Zondervan, 2019), 417.

the unregenerate. Paul didn't isolate himself around other believers. Do you want a self-reflective question? How many unregenerate (non-believers) people do you personally know and interact with on a daily basis? How many do you actively have natural gospel conversations with? If your answer is none or minimal, you may begin realizing why you're not making reproducible disciple-makers.

Let's get back to the Apostle Paul. I find it amazing how the church has traditionally viewed Paul through the lens of mission without attaching him to how he received an income. Paul is always viewed as a church planter, a missionary, or an Apostle, yet, his vocation was tentmaker. Paul didn't rely on the church to produce his means for living.

The reality is, Paul declared, "If anyone is not willing to work, let him not eat." (2 Thess. 3:10b). That's pretty harsh. I'm not saying that pastoral clergy do not work—some work upwards of 60-hour weeks and always are on call. But, Paul commanded the newly gathered saints to be working people—to work among their community.

In Paul's mindset, he was more than willing *not* to accept any wages for fulfilling the mission of God (Phil. 4:17). With that said, I'm not an "either/or" type person, I believe that God has gifted some people to be pastors and teachers, while others are to be pioneers—of the apostolic kind. However, with that said, since the culture has shifted from the church to the marketplace, I also envision a time coming, very soon, when the pastoral salaried positions will be left by the wayside. The result will be a majority need for bi-vocations, regardless. For this reason, I love

Southeastern Baptist Theological Seminary as they train leaders for business and church planting—a much needed training.

I am often asked by planters, "Should I go to seminary and get a Masters of Divinity degree?" I always answer in the same way, and this by experience. "No, I think you should get an MBA, and be discipled in theology, mission, ecclesiology, and doctrine. Then once you're in the marketplace, if you still feel that you need more theological training, strive for a divinity degree." Why? I say this because a paradigm shift has occurred and we're not returning to the old way of life.

So, let's begin our bi-vocational church planting journey with Anchor Trades.

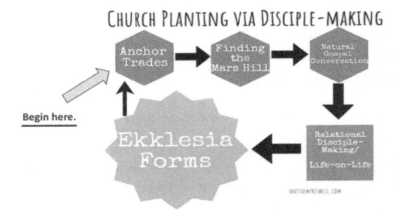

Anchor Trades

Undoubtedly, one of the greatest stressors that planters endure seems to be a financial one. While many planters can and should seek funding by receiving partner support, they will inevitably become bi-vocational, needing to earn an income. I have been bi-vocational for over 10 years, so what I'm introducing is not theory, but praxis. So, in my opinion, Anchor Trades are the best way to be bi-vocational and to be an effective RDM.

I'll explain Anchor Trades and what they are momentarily. But, to establish a successful Anchor Trade, the planter should perform research about the new community to understand the culture. I would recommend actively walking the geographic location months prior to planning, not only to make an assessment, but also to put your pulse on the community and how it thrives. Next, as the planter seeks that vocation, they should allow a healthy balance of income and community engagement. This is where most planters fail.

Unfortunately, most planters who are bi-vocational are trying to support a family at the same time, so they tend to seek out an occupation where they can earn the greatest amount of money. Can you fault them? Absolutely not. Others desire to have a vocation prior to planting, but it may keep the planter from community engagement, which is critical. So, there is a way to develop a healthy balance between maximizing the planters' exposure to the community for impact *and* maximizing the income potential within a specific vocation. The expectations may not be what the planter anticipates, but again, the cost of discipleship is the Christ-life.

Anchor Trade. What is it? The term Anchor Trade is a specific expression that I coined. It's a comprehensive term that refers to effective bi-vocational occupations for church planters. As I stated, most planters make the mistake of trying to maximize their income, but the end result minimizes their exposure to the community.[120] Most of the passionate planters that I have known will ask the question: How can I be obedient to the Great Commission while earning an income?

One of the most effective ways that I have witnessed is the Anchor Trade—a vocation that is steeped within a community (i.e. anchored). For example, the Apostle Paul was a tentmaker (Acts 18:3). The tentmaker profession during the First Century makes a good illustration of an Anchor Trade vocation because it directly serves and meets a need within its community. The trade is a vocation that is "anchored" within a specific culture.

However, Anchor Trades are called trades, not jobs. Why? If planters are passionate about reaching their community, they understand that mission is who we are and not what we do. The church does not have a mission, but the mission has a church (I think Alan Hirsch said that, but I can't find it. Regardless, it's not mine). Anyway, Anchor Trades are purposefully twofold. A trade is a vocation to earn an income and a trade is usually a vocation that has an apprentice.

Some examples of modern Anchor Trades may include a barber/hair stylist, chimney sweeper, HVAC technician, computer repair (shared space), mechanic, landscaper,

---

120 The first time that I heard of maximizing and minimizing was from Peyton Jones. When I was the Executive Director of New Breed, Peyton and I would have discussions regarding assisting church planters in being effective at bi-vocational living. Peyton originated the terminology of maximizing community exposure and the popular minimization of income. Jones, Peyton. New Breed Church Planting. 2014.

teacher, or entrepreneur, to name a few. To reiterate, to establish a successful Anchor Trade, the planter should perform on-the-ground research about the new community to understand the community/city, actively walk it to make an assessment, and seek a vocation that will allow a healthy balance of income and community engagement. You're not looking for the highest paid position, or the lowest paid, but one that you will be able to earn an income to provide and also have natural gospel conversations with unregenerate peoples.

Let me address another church planter failure. Some planters assume that all they need to do is show up—utilizing an attractional method (i.e. If you build it, they will come). But failing to perform research, assessments, and community engagements prior to arriving in a new community is not a good strategy. They rely on hope, and, as the Navy SEALS say, "Hope is a terrible strategy."

As the diagram below illustrates, combining the best social media campaigns, mailers, billboards, road signs, newspaper ads, door-to-door knocking, and internet communication do not equal or compare to the impact of personal relationships. Church planting takes intentionality and time—it is *never* to be rushed. Allow the Spirit to go as fast or slow as He wills. Some planters expect explosive growth, but singular church planters (I'll address this term shortly) should map out a real strategy with quantifiable metrics. But, don't lose sight of what God may be doing in relation to having to adapt strategies. We'll talk more about strategies in the REAPSOW section.

Back when I was with New Breed Church Planting Network,[121] I labeled (and coined) certain jobs as Anchor Trades due to the trades' ability to meet a community's need and the possibility of having the greatest amount of exposure to lostness. While most people don't think about their jobs in this way, plumbers, barbers, store clerks, chimney sweeps, builders, and even IT gurus are being utilized in this manner. The mission field isn't the church, but the community and the occupation in which one is gifted for employment.

At New Breed, we looked at the Anchor Trade disciple-making opportunity as a two-fold. Not only would a bi-vocational planter make disciples of Christ within their profession by meeting new converts, but he also had an opportunity to disciple *within* the trade. The planter learns or teaches the trade to someone else. Cultivating these gospel trades is a term that I use to identify a profession in which a person can teach a trade in tandem with making gospel-centered disciples. I perceive that the Apostle did this with Timothy and Silas, possibly teaching them tent-making while also teaching them how to live out a Christ-centered faith. It is highly plausible that Timothy had his own vocation, but I like to think that Paul showed him the ropes of tent-making (pun intended).

What does that look like for us? For instance, if I'm hired as a wood worker and have a few helpers to build a table, while we're fastening the sides of a table together, I may begin to explain how the Holy Spirit works within

---

121 New Breed is a global church planting network, specifically designed as a super-collective existing of many denominations. See https://newbreednetwork.org

my life to build stability. May I express how the wood reminds me of the cross of Christ, bringing humanity and God together? Or perhaps, if I'm sanding down the top, I may suggest that sometimes God places people in our lives that act as our "sandpaper"—somewhat abrasive—but developing our maturity in Christ-like humility. Regardless, hopefully you get the picture of natural gospel conversations.

Mostly, I believe that any profession can be rendered into a cultivated gospel trade. But I think our perception of the term "job" connotes a negative one. It assumes the daily grind, hated Mondays and glorious Fridays. But Anchor Trades should be viewed as gospel empowering positions of mission. While the planter is teaching the trade itself, he's also making disciple-makers. These are merely two of the ways in which bi-vocational planters can better engage in disciple-making, but it's certainly not exhaustive.

Shared Spaces

Perhaps, this section should be placed within the Church Planting chapter, but I believe it fits better associated with Anchor Trades and bi-vocational ministry. As stated, knowing that the culture has shifted from the church building to the marketplace has led many church planters into spared spaces. Shared spaces are nothing new, planters have been utilizing shared spaces for years, most likely, and not even realizing that God's working hand was bringing them to the forefront of the frontier. Planters are pioneers.

I happen to love shared spaces and am currently planting out of one. Most singular church planting occurs within a shared space. Recently, the big picture is coming into more focus. The Covid-19 pandemic has proven this strategy to be a bit more successful than the traditional one of owning a space/building. When a church body makes the shift from shared space to owned building, it seems that a systemic change occurs. The people become focused on maintaining and using the building, instead of missional impact. So, I find the shared space more effective. As well, the location of the shared space is within the community. This means that the space already has foot traffic.

Our shared space happens to be a CrossFit gym called Pride Fitness, a privately-owned facility. Story church began our relationship building with Vec when we partnered with Pride Fitness (then Soldier Fit) to bless the military community. Vec designed a demanding and grueling course with twelve obstacles—called Warrior's Way—the last obstacle was to pull an actual monster truck! And, yes, I was the oldest to compete, but the event was not for Story Church, we were the sponsor. We had competing teams, paid for the food truck, advertising, needs, and organized the use of the grounds for the event.

We've partnered with Pride Fitness to not only help them in their altruistic endeavors of blessing the community, but also in serving and getting to know their members. Truly, our shared space is a Mars Hill—the Hampton Roads community breathes fitness. While Story Church is focused on the military community, Pride Fitness presented an excellent opportunity for us to meet the military community of Virginia Beach. It was an opportunity that we otherwise would not have had.

Let me briefly share a "God-story" with you. From the inception of Story Church, Jonathan and I had planned on the Story Church movement to use shared spaces near military communities. Fast forward to post Warrior's Way. About one month later, I felt like God was prodding me back into the business field. I had an inner urge to become a business owner again, maybe own a gym, and plant Story church out of it (Story Church had no home at the time). So, I texted Vec. I asked him if we could meet the next day. I wanted to share with him what was on my heart and get some insight about owning a gym-business.

The next day I show up at Vec's gym. We sat down and I began to unload my heart. The entire time he's patiently listening. That's when God blew me away. Vec looked me in the eye and said, "Hey, don't think this is weird or anything, but God told me why you're here."

I was caught off guard. As I had a conversation with myself, I began to think, "Ok, I got to hear this!" because I know how God works.

Vec continues, "God told me that you're looking for a place. So, how about if Story Church comes into this facility? You can use it on Sundays all day while no one is here. It's all yours. If you need more time, let me know." And like that—Vec and I have been brothers and Story Church has a shared-space home.

Anyway, I had stated earlier that an Anchor Trade could be a computer savvy person and I suspect someone reading this may wonder how. When I was the Executive Director of New Breed, we had a church planter in Spain who was a computer guru—at least to me, he was. He began his church planting journey finding that Anchor Trade. As he started to work in a facility that had multiple companies and ample space, he eventually got to know some of the people and invited them over his house. Eventually, he asked management if he could utilize the facility when it was not being used. He got the OK. This is just another example of how shared spaces are a great way to make an impact upon a community.

Currently, there are church planters all over the world beginning businesses for this specific reason. Some planters become entrepreneurs, owning the gym, coffee shop, or whatever it may be. But, I believe that shared spaces will be the future of the church, just as Anchor Trades will be. While some people view shared spaces as completely missional, I would state that there is still an attractional aspect of church gatherings that shared spaces employ. However, there should be a greater benefit with gathering within a community business setting instead of being viewed as the church building on the corner.

What might one of those benefits be? I believe the greatest benefit of gathering in shared spaces relates to real life. Shared spaces are where life happens each and every day—it's the marketplace. If reproducible disciple-making is the goal, then life-on-life must exist.

Navigating Church Planting

Fact: You cannot understand what you do not know.

I f you're reading this work, most likely you have ventured down the path of church planting, had a person suggest that you research church planting, or maybe you know someone who is church planting. Either way, church planting relates to the frontlines of gospel ministry—it's about redemptively engaging lostness within the subcultures of society. Currently, there are many differing opinions, models, and strategies concerning church planting—far different than the days of Bob Logan's *Church Planter Toolkit* (which is still the bomb).[122]

One of the reasons for the differing strategies of church planting correlates with the rapid change of culture. Not unlike the paradigm shifting of large technological organizations or mammoth-sized businesses, inevitable change, innovation, and adaptability must occur within the church. While the gospel never changes, the habits, values, norms, and beliefs of societies do. Hence, the great need for developing and implementing appropriate strategies for

---

122 Logan, Robert, E. *The Church Planter's Toolkit.* https://www.amazon.com/Church-Planters-Toolkit-Robert-Logan/dp/1889638080.

reaching lostness. However, as Peter Drucker (supposedly) famously quipped, "Culture eats strategy for breakfast."[123]

Should church planters be fearful of ever-changing hungry culture(s)? Of course, the answer to that question is—absolutely not. As believers in Christ, we should be utilizing the underlying concepts of *how* and *why* our culture is eating our strategy. Yet, "The cross births a new people who view themselves as equals, because they are reconciled to Christ and to one another," culminating in a cruciform community of believers.[124] The church can navigate culture, as Jesus noted, "For the sons of this world are more shrewd in dealing with their own generation than the sons of light" (Luke 16:8b). Church planters should be cognizant of culture.

In understanding culture, I believe the concepts and principles of biblical church planting usually relate to what I call, the four respective—"uns"—an un-saved and un-known people whereby the planter abides in an un-familiar and un-engaged culture. These four "uns" should propel believers to become obedient Great Commission-driven disciple-makers. As the Apostle Paul declared, "For the love of Christ controls us…" (2 Cor. 5:14).

Disciple-makers of Christ must not lose focus on the purpose and risks of church planting, which is, Great Commission obedience (Matt. 28:18–20). By being obedient risk-takers, church planters face the daily rhythms

---

123 Quoteinvestigator.com. Peter F. Drucker. May 23, 2017. https://quoteinvestigator.com/2017/05/23/culture-eats/

124 Gray, Derwin, L. *The High Definition Leader: Building Multiethnic Churches in a Multiethnic* World (Nashville: Thomas Nelson, 2015), 50.

of the four "uns" along with an ever-present fifth "un" — the reality of un-certainty. There is always a looming uncertainty of success or failure, which adds to the daily pressures (2 Cor. 11:28).

While there is no lack of church planting materials to help planters face some of the uncertainty of what lies ahead, most articles and books advise against planting churches solo. However, the greatest percentage of church planters is marital teams. Regardless of whether your spouse is thinking about planting, they will be planting with you, once the step is made. So, let me be brutally honest, if your wife has not been called to church planting, you have not been called, either. I say this from experience. Your marriage will be destroyed. Church planting is one of the loneliest, most depressing, and difficult tasks, but its obedient reward is worth all of the risks. Success is not numbers or growth, success is obedience.

So, let's get back to the four "uns". They will always be evident, whether or not the marital church planting team, as Priscilla and Aquila (Acts 18:26; Rom. 16:3; 1 Cor. 16:19), has partner-sponsors, a mother church, denominational support, or an ample number of committed "boot-camp" workshops to attend. The material that you're about to read will help you navigate through the uncertain waters of the four "uns". Remember, there is no red bat, but we can create adaptable strategy.

The Four Uns

Sometimes church planters will use labels like cultural exegesis or contextualization, at least, I do. The former refers to understanding a specific culture (and sub-culture) and the setting, while the latter refers to the application(s) and proclamation of the gospel. We understand that language barriers exist as even within the same language, there may be dialect issues.

I grew up in New York, which was a far cry from where my parents grew up in Virginia. As I grew older and listened to my friends, neighbors, and teachers, I realized that my mother had a different way of speaking along with clichés, colloquialisms, and sayings. I still have no idea what "more than I can shake a stick at" means.

In the same manner, church planters should understand that certain behaviors, values of life, rituals, religions, and living arrangements can be quite different—even within our own city and town limits. I believe that these four "uns" exist in nearly every cultural setting. Embracing those four "uns" will help the planter in identifying and implementing the best strategies for Great Commission obedience (Matt. 28:18–20). I have labeled the four "uns" as un-saved, un-known, un-familiar, and un-engaged.

As I've stated, I firmly believe that singular church planting is one of the most effective ways for connecting with (1) unsaved people; (2) building gospel relationships within an unknown society; (3) making disciples in an unfamiliar location; and (4) impacting an unengaged culture with the power of Christ—*if*—it is done intentionally.

Singular planting does not refer to the number of church plants, as in multiplication, but concerns the individual strategy and nature of a specific type of church plant. Singular church planting explicitly relates to the number of people (i.e. married couple or individual) that seeks to start a new church. Sometimes this terminology is better known as "parachute planting."

I prefer the term singular church planting, because I don't think people can relate to jumping out of an airplane. I also perceive that many believers have a fearful conception of doing so. Sure, church planting is difficult, and I'll mention those aspects of being behind enemy lines, but I'm always seeking the most biblical strategy that I can find. Singular church planting refers to the biblical strategies that are utilized within the Scriptures and in our modern culture and consists of a team of 1 to 4 people. Sure, it may seem like semantics, and maybe it is, but it helps me to understand what needs to be done and the certain strategies to be employed.

What is the difference between singular church planting and some of the other church planting models? Generally speaking, it's all about people. In my opinion, if you send out 50 people to "plant" a church, you're not actually planting a new church—you already have a church. That number of people is a church re-location. However, for the Great Commission to be accomplished, I am not an either/or type believer, but a both/and—meaning, the church will need a multi-pronged approach to reach the lostness in Western culture. So, go ahead and send your fifty people, just keep RDMs as the main goal.

With that being stated, the majority of singular church plants will fail within the first three years—much like any business. Typically, singular planters come from a different geographical context (ethnic, socio-economic, cultural), they relocate their entire family to an unsaved people group, settle in within an unknown society, become part of an unfamiliar place, and have to comprehend a new unengaged culture. Sometimes this causes "culture shock" and isolation.

Unsaved people in an unknown and an unfamiliar culture that are unengaged are the underpinnings of a disciple-making ethos. Beginning with unregenerate people and introducing their culture or sub-culture to the King of all creation is an exciting venture. There will be challenges, for sure, but studying all of the four "uns" will better serve the planter in engagement. I would recommend that a planter whiteboard the four "uns" of their potential location. Think strategies, not model. Strategies are always adaptable; most models are not. While whiteboarding, think as if you were one of the "uns". Immerse yourself in creatively connecting with the people.

One of the greatest pieces of advice I would give to a potential church planter is to not create something that isn't meant to be. Many singular planters impatiently develop liturgies way before they ever set foot in the city. If your main motive is to bring a specific liturgy to a sub-culture, you've missed the target.

God has created us to be intelligent and creative. As a semi-avid reader, I love reading differing books. Maybe they're business related, about culture, economics, or history.

One book that I enjoyed was *Creating Great Choices*. The authors Riel and Martin present applicable insight into integrative thinking. In correlation with waiting to see how God wants to impact a certain people and what manner of heart worship could be utilized, there's a statement in the book that says, "Listening only to those who agree with us reinforces our existing views, blinds us to the flaws in our reasoning, and limits the creativity of our thinking."[125] You get the point.

And so, if most singular church plants die within the first three years, it's surprising that most *successful* singular church planters endure by embedding themselves inside a community, within the first three years. For this reason, singular church planters should embrace a Great Commission mindset that consists of RDM strategies. Engaging the unengaged is essential and obedient.

Behind Enemy Lines

One time when I was with New Breed, I was flown into California to gather with some of the guys. I always loved going out to southern California—it reminds me of my days in the Navy. The weather is nearly identical every day and enjoyable. Plus, New Breeders truly are a different breed of people. I love those West Coast guys!

Anyway, New Breed had several church planters in the Huntington Beach area—they were (and still are) pioneers and bold witnesses for Jesus Christ. New Breed paid for

---

125 Riel, Jennifer, and Roger L. Martin, *Creating Great Choices: A leader's Guide to Integrative Thinking* (Boston: Harvard Business Review, 2017), 79.

my visit and put me up in a hotel that was in the midst and heart of an area that was desperately in need of the gospel. If you were to take a quick glance at Huntington Beach, everything would look healthy and normal from an appearance standpoint, but underneath all of the car dealerships and businesses was a dark side—the drugs, homelessness, and high crime. This is why I always loved New Breeders—they went to places that no one else wanted to go.

After I checked-in, I had a few hours of alone time, so I decided to do some reconnoitering. I always like to walk around an area that I've never been to before. I've been to southern California, but not this part of Huntington Beach. So, I walked directly behind the hotel, in the alleyway between businesses. It was there that I met a homeless man pushing his life's belongings in an old beat up shopping cart. He was very closed-off and didn't want to talk to me. Even after I confided in him that I was a pastor, he said that no church ever accepted him or helped him.

After over an hour of talking, I was able to share the love of Christ with him and he seemed responsive—I wasn't overly pushy. It so happens that the same alley with the homeless man was directly underneath my window. And the next event to happen, I will always remember.

Unfortunately, as I was sleeping that night, about 2 a.m., I awoke to hearing someone running toward my window. I heard a scuffling taking place—then—he gurgled cries—a person was being stabbed right under my window. I heard it all—time was in slow motion—the dramatic footsteps, the shrieking, and the cries of the victim to stop. I would say it was horrifying, and it was, but unfortunately, I think we have become a culture accustomed to death. I do have to say that the police responded faster than I have ever witnessed; within minutes. Anyway, I felt a deep burden for Huntington Beach. I placed my face in my hands, and intensely prayed for this lost and broken world.

One of my favorite movie series is HBO's *Band of Brothers*, written about Easy Company from the 101st Airborne and their World War II missions from D-Day to VE Day.[126] In one particular scene, when they're about to enter the Bastogne region, Captain Winters is warned about what lies ahead for his Easy Company.

A Lieutenant pipes up, "Sir, you and your men are behind enemy lines, you're going to be surrounded."

Winters retorts, "We're Paratroopers, soldier, we're supposed to be surrounded."

So, early the next morning, my friend Peyton picked me up for some coffee and conversation. I confided in him about what had occurred the day prior with the homeless man and about what had happened with the stabbing during the night. He apologized about the area and said, "Man, I'm sorry that you had to experience all that."

I asserted, "Bro, it's all good—we're church planters, we're supposed to be surrounded."

I think sometimes believers need to be reminded that this world is not our home. Any ground that we advance

---

126 Ambrose. Band of Brothers. New York: HBO Home Entertainment, 2010.

the kingdom into is enemy territory—but not in the sense of people. No, instead, there's a spiritual enemy that has us in his crosshairs (Eph. 6:12). While we're surrounded by the lostness and brokenness of people, church planters are specifically called as God's "elite force" for engaging enemy lines—to engage the forces of evil—surrounded by an invisible enemy.

Even though God is sovereign and owns every square millimeter of creation, the Scriptures reveal that a war is occurring (Eph. 6:10–12). I wanted to clarify the point of enemy lines and being surrounded because believers, and especially church planters, ought always to "count the cost" (Luke 14:28). There should never be any grandiose expectations of an easy, glamorous, or respected position. Church planting is grunt life, lay-down-your-life-style obedience, but if we do it right, making disciple-makers, we're not really planting churches, we're establishing possible generations of redeemed people.

Church planting is not for everyone. While many believers like the *idea* of church planting, it's not for the faint of heart. The reality is that it can be an extremely lonely and difficult war that takes place on the front lines of lostness—and along the way there are many spiritual battles—and more often than not, you will lose some comrades along the way, but, hopefully, you will gain some new ones.

Lastly, I would be doing the planter a disservice if I didn't provide another truth. That core group of people that you're so excited about—they're probably going to leave. It is what it is. Don't think of it as betrayal. Many planters get emotionally hurt and feel abandoned. On the contrary, look at the positive and be glad that you had them for a time period. God will always provide you with the right individuals, and many, if you're abiding by the principles that Jesus put forth.

I believe the parable of the talents (Matt. 25) is a good example of disciple-making. If the Great Commission is the command given to believers—to go and make other disciples—then we should expect to hear the question one day: "How many disciples did you make?" Hopefully, the answer will be however many people the Lord gave to you. "Lord, I have made twenty disciples," you will say.

Maybe the Lord responds, "Well done, good and faithful servant. You have been faithful over a little; I will set you over much." Regardless, I do believe that we will give an account of our disciple-making because that was the one command we were given. I hope by this point, you have established a decent understanding of RDM. I'd like to lastly move to the RDM strategy for planters that I believe is a good plan of attack—always be on the offensive.

Finding the Mars Hill

Assuming that the singular planter has become employed within an Anchor Trade, what's the next step for me? I believe that the planter should locate the community's Mars Hill. Finding the "Mars Hill" is extremely important — something that all missionaries completely understand. I think sometimes planters forget about the journey, the process of engaging people groups and communities.

In Acts 17, Luke records that while Paul was waiting for his church planting team to arrive that his "spirit was provoked within him" (Acts 17:16). It seems logical that

Paul went for a walk and reconnoitered the city of Athens. He was walking around looking at all of the statues molded into foreign gods. His later conversation with the Stoic and Epicurean philosophers reveals that he had discovered the Athenians "Mars Hill." So, for this reason, I began labeling the concept of exegeting the community to specifically decipher what unreached peoples worshipped as, the Mars Hill. It is the Mars Hill, in which a planter who has established an Anchor Trade should start.

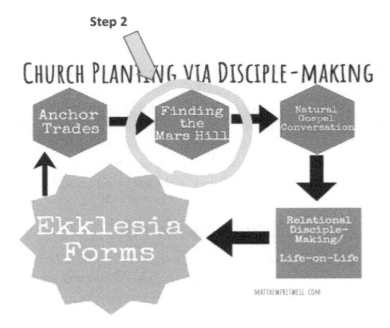

Again, utilizing one of the Apostle Paul's greatest recorded gospel contextualization conversations (Acts 17:16–31), Mars Hill refers to what a community or culture worships. For the planter, what he really needs to know is what do the people idolize and what can they *not*

do without? It is essential and imperative for the singular planter to locate the Mars Hill. It will be how the people relate and speak. It is the pulse of the community.

Finding the Mars Hill also correlates to locating the subcultures within a specific community, neighborhood, or city. Sub-cultures are where life happens. I have a document that I provide for my students and planters. In the document, I have listed nearly every possible subculture. The reason for finding the Mars Hill is not to know it, but to engage it. As I stated earlier, you cannot understand what you do not know.

So, why subcultures?

A subculture is a part of a society that has similar norms, values, and interests. They do life together in and through interactive and engageable daily rhythms, existing in a greater culture. Subcultures have shared ideology, aesthetics, and language. Think of subcultures as cliques, or people that engage in the same passions. Think skateboarders, goth, LGBTQ, CrossFit, runners, etc. Each of these subcultures exists within a greater culture. Learning that there's a running subculture does the planter no good unless there's a strategy to engage it.

For example, I remember one planter that I helped utilize the Mars Hill principle. He, indeed, had a running culture in his town. He was trying to find a way to impact it, but the running clubs met and ran on Sunday mornings, when he was trying to congregate his small church plant (another reason why earlier I stated to wait on God before you formulate what he may want to achieve through you).

I advised this planter for his church plant to sponsor a 5k. I also advised him to connect with as many local businesses as he could to get partners for T-Shirts, prizes (coupons, gift certificates, etc.), and volunteers. This is how to engage a subculture.

Going back to what I presented earlier about creativity, I know that most planters are visionaries, but that vision has to become creative to put things into application. Engagement should be the result of finding the Mars Hill. Think "outside the box." There are literally hundreds of subcultures in the United States. What would happen if each church had small groups that adopted a subculture within its community and engaged it? Would the church become diverse over time? Absolutely. So, the object is not to find one sole Mars Hill, but to continually engage multiple Mars Hills. The more that can be identified and reached, the greater will be the RDM probability. Below is a practical diagram of neighborhood mapping (something I really haven't addressed, but it's phenomenal at building relationships), Anchor Trades, Finding the Mars Hill, and natural gospel conversations.

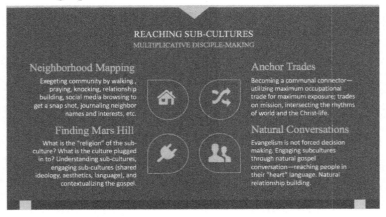

REACHING SUB-CULTURES
MULTIPLICATIVE DISCIPLE-MAKING

Neighborhood Mapping
Exegeting community by walking, praying, knocking, relationship building, social media browsing to get a snap shot, journaling neighbor names and interests, etc.

Anchor Trades
Becoming a communal connector—utilizing maximum occupational trade for maximum exposure; trades on mission, intersecting the rhythms of world and the Christ-life.

Finding Mars Hill
What is the "religion" of the subculture? What is the culture plugged in to? Understanding sub-cultures, engaging sub-cultures (shared ideology, aesthetics, language), and contextualizing the gospel.

Natural Conversations
Evangelism is not forced decision making. Engaging subcultures through natural gospel conversation—reaching people in their "heart" language. Natural relationship building.

REAPSOW: RDM
Church Planting Praxis

I n this last chapter, the longest, I want to explore a way to get back to our biblical roots — to be sent out as RDMs (reproducible disciple-makers), to learn how to revitalize and plant churches through multiplicative disciple-making. My hope is that you will also learn how to make an impact on your community by effectively navigating through it.

Admittedly, REAPSOW began as a strategy project for my doctoral work. When I was going through my oral arguments stage, my doctoral review board prodded me to put this in print. However, while humbled, I agreed, but with the exception that at least two generations had to be reproduced. I never wanted to be a theory guy. So, REAPSOW is developed as a practical and adaptable guide to reaching and creating RDMs from the four "uns" (un-saved, un-known, un-familiar, and un-engaged). I've taught this strategy to pastors, churches (for revitalization) and planters, and I'm also currently using it.

While I certainly praise God for all church planting efforts, I believe that the church needs to approach church planting from every possible angle. The fact is that the majority of church planting is not done with $100,000. It's also not achieved with a high capacity missional group of fifty to a hundred people. Likewise, by sending a group of fifty or even a hundred people into a city, a DNA of the "church" already exists and most likely will not become indigenous. Don't get me wrong, as I've professed, I'm not against it, I'm all for it, but it is what it is.

For the current church to see multiplicative growth, I believe it needs to persistently stay focused upon a comprehensive approach to reproducible communal disciple-making. As we've already noted, the reality is that more churches are planted by singular church planting. For this reason, REAPSOW was designed with a developed and purposeful intent of singular church planting efforts, for maximum impact. With that stated, maximum impact does not mean numerical growth, but creating RDMs. Success isn't about generating or sustaining members but making disciple-makers.

Consequently, what you're about to read is a look into REAPSOW—a reproducible disciple-making strategy that I designed and have applied to church planting. With seven sub-tilted headings for examining each aspect of the REAPSOW praxis, you should be able to develop and engage your community, city, or neighborhood. As well, if you're wondering why REAP is before SOW, it's because REAPSOW was intentionally designed "backwards," with the sowing part listed after reaping. I believe we need to plant churches backwards. We shouldn't be trying to create an atmosphere and environment for making disciples, but make disciples that end up developing and establishing an environment for gathering.

But, why is REAPSOW really backwards? This is because disciple-making already exists. The goal is reaching new converts to help them yearn for the presence of an amazing God who will then make other disciple-makers. To clarify and answer the age-old question, the chicken came before the egg.

Beginning an adaptable strategy must start with those passionate about reaching, teaching, and living among the lost. As one of my favorite quotes from Antoine de Saint-Exupery says, "If you want to build a ship, don't summon people to buy wood, prepare tools, distribute jobs, and organize the work, rather teach people the yearning for a wide, boundless ocean." I passionately desire that you would come to know the unconditional love and grace of Christ and follow Him as he leads you on His Great Commission (Matt. 28:18–20).

I want you think of REAPSOW as an *overlapping* seven-unit "practicum," designed to strategically and practically make reproducible disciple-makers from new converts. As Hirsch clarifies, "Discipleship is both critical and strategic."[127] What REAPSOW is *not*, is a program to be completed. You're not going to get a gold star. Rather, it's an *adaptable* guideline to engage in life-on-life witness for spiritual maturity in Christ.

The seven elements of REAPSOW are: (1) **R**eaching New Converts; (2) **E**quipping as Church; (3) **A**ssisting in Mentorship; (4) **P**racticing the Presence of Christ; (5) **S**pirit Empowerment; (6) **O**bedient Living; and (7) **W**itness in

---

127 Hirsch, *The Forgotten Ways*, 111.

Withness. The first letter of each concept is used to create an acronym to help remember certain aspects for RDM development.

Reaching New Converts

As I researched the biblical passage and formation of Matt. 28:18–20 and Acts 1:8, it became apparent to begin the disciple-making process with evangelism to new converts. I know some believers like to divorce evangelism from disciple-making—I'm not one of those people. I think like Derwin Gray who says, "When worship is a lifestyle, evangelism is not an activity but an identity."[128] In all honesty, I believe that there is no discipleship without evangelism. You can have evangelism without discipleship, but not vice versa. Why?

Great Commission disciple-making requires the proclamation of the gospel. I think too many times, the Western Church, as we discussed in chapter two, has been brainwashed into thinking that discipleship is a class, a program, or a development process for believers only. Contrary to that belief, discipleship begins prior to conversion—it begins in building the relationship. Discipleship is not solely about conversion, profession, or salvation.

We can ultimately agree that disciple-making begins at relationship. It's obvious. Jesus selected Judas and considered him a disciple—one can assume that Judas never was illuminated, never regenerated, and never redeemed—yet

---

128 Gray, *The High Definition Leader*, 115.

he was always considered a disciple by Jesus (Matt. 10:1–4). This, too, is something that we've already discussed in a previous chapter, so no need to reiterate.

For church planters, they would do well to strive to transform their community by forming a body of Christ through disciple-making. We know biblically that the church is symbolically related to a body, we even call it the corporate body (Rom. 12:5). Imagine a newborn infant, yet prior to its birth, it is being formed with important parts within the mother's womb—these are essential parts like organs: heart, lungs, liver, kidneys, brain, and nervous system. The body of the infant must go through a development stage prior to birth, if not, the baby will most likely have deformity issues. Likewise, if church planters seek to start with a building prior to the disciple-making formation, they risk deformity, immaturity, and a lack for reproducible DNA.

In my opinion, all church planters should plant pregnant. Planting pregnant already assumes the DNA of multiplication. When I designed REAPSOW, I intentionally thought of it a means to apprentice (disciple by example) another planter by having them experientially learn to understand the subcultural settings of the city/community by watching a lead planter. For this reason, I may use the term apprentice interchangeably with disciple-maker (in essence, that's what we're doing, except we're creating disciples of Jesus, not us. They watch and imitate us, as we watch and imitate Christ).

So, to *reach new converts* (**R**), the apprentice and planter (if planting pregnant) must know the community.

You cannot reach what you do not know. Much like the Apostle Paul in Athens (Acts 17:16), planters should seek out the Mars Hill of the city—what do the people worship? One way to learn about the people within the city is via applied demographics, by walking the streets of the community and seeking out natural gospel conversations. Demographics are mere numbers, while useful in many ways, they're useless unless they're applied.

Honestly, church planters that I've known are really good at researching demographics and psychographics, but perhaps poor at applied demographics which is the use of the tools employed to better understand and engage the people you're trying to reach. As Paul walked through Athens, he noted that the Athenians were worshippers of many gods (Acts 17:16). Paul used his religious "demographic" information for gospel proclamation. Applied demographics are essential to truly knowing the lostness and subcultures of communities/cities for the proclamation and living out of the gospel.

Previously, I mentioned Anchor Trades. An Anchor Trade is one of the best ways to utilize applied demographics because you become a working part of the community. As relationships are formed, discipleship begins. What does the "R" truly look like applied?

The church planter actively engages and applies the aspects of natural gospel conversations within everyday life. You want to proclaim the gospel and allow its working power by the Spirit to engage and transform the unregenerate. Natural gospel conversations are those not based upon coercion, but dialogue, reflection, intrigue, and relationship.

One of my favorite movie scenes is from *The Princess Bride*. Inigo Montoya is frustratingly waiting for Wesley to climb the Cliffs of Insanity. As soon as Wesley is to ascend to the top, Inigo will challenge him to a sword duel. The entertainment happens when Wesley reaches the top and sits down to take a rock out of his boot.

Inigo impatiently prods him, "You don't by any chance have six fingers on your left hand?"

Wesley humorously responds, "Do you always begin conversations this way?"

A very funny scene, but the church has been so methodically programmed to think in "Christianese," or to "complete the sale," that it has forgotten how to have natural gospel conversations. Church planters are no different. The first words from planters' mouths should not be, "Are you saved?" This is a question that unregenerate people have no concept of. It should, "Hi, my name is _____, how are you?"

Discipleship begins with natural gospel conversations — not at a person's conversion. This means that a planter must be incarnational within the community. Learning to exegete the area of the potential plant is imperative, but so is the essentiality of building strong business and community-wide relationships. To reach new converts, the planter must think as the unregenerate and engage their Mars Hill — truly seeking to find out what they're worshipping. Don't worry, they'll let you know as they talk. This means active listening is part of the conversation.

I've taught some church planters within their cities to use their smart phones to log information. Sometimes it's useful for those with memory problems, like me. As they enter an unfamiliar store (one of the "uns"), they should greet those who work there. Ask them how they're doing — get to know them — do they have kids, are they in college, preschool, how long have they lived in the area, how long have they worked at that store etc. The idea is not to be a creeper, but to log all of the information that you can, presumably, after you leave. You're not a journalist taking notes, just merely collecting information to build relationships.

The next time you enter the store, when you meet that same individual, you now have something to ask to begin the conversation (i.e. how are your kids? How was your long drive in this morning? How is your schooling going? I was thinking about you.). While these things sound meaningless, they're imperative in applied demographics. A city's demographic may tell you people's religion, ages, ethnicities, and incomes, but not who they are.

What if by asking your questions, the person shares inside information with you? What if they tell you one of their kids is sick, their car is having problems, and they can't afford their tuition? This is how natural gospel conversations are developed and relationships are built — by sharing and caring.

A church planter should actively strive to reach unchurched people within their city via gospel-centered focus on natural evangelism (i.e. building relationship with unregenerate people). Relationship-building is practicality. And, one of the most sensible methods of getting to know the community has the planter recording the names, conversations, and stories of people he/she engages. You can also use this principle for neighborhood mapping.

So, inevitably, the next time the planter engages in conversation with the person of interest, there's a first name basis and a background. Marketplace atmospheres are some of the best areas for engaging unregenerate people. Locating the places where a community gathers and associates with one another becomes vital in the *Reaching* "phase." As the planter becomes comfortable and effective with their community "mapping" strategies, they will unavoidably unveil new subcultures.

Subcultural places can exist as tattoo parlors, skate parks, cross-fit gymnasiums, cigar lounges, or coffee houses. I happen to like the cigar lounge. Once a person lights up, he or she is there for an hour, at least. Inevitably, they will ask me, 'What do you do?" And, game on!

But, any establishment in which unregenerate people may gather with similar likes and dislikes can assist the planter in engaging in natural gospel conversations with potential new converts. This is one of the reasons why I love planting pregnant—I literally have the ability to walk a potential planter through the process of relationship building, creating natural gospel conversations, and reaching new converts. But, one of the goals for this phase is actually having a person submit their life to Christ; then you can enter into the next phase of this RDM strategy.

Equip as the Church

According to the Great Commission, Jesus commanded his disciples to baptize new converts in the name of the "Father, Son, and Holy Spirit" (Matt. 28:19). New converts become identified with Christ through baptism into his body, the church, for the equipping of ministry (Eph. 4:11–14). Ministry relates specifically to the church and its mission.

In the *Equip as Church* (**E**) "practicum," the planter teaches the new convert the importance of submission to Christ, baptismal identity, servanthood, church membership, and the unity of the body of Christ for service. As well, the convert is told about the mission of God and how the person fits within the corporate body become essential. The new believer that you're now discipling needs to know, by example, the power of God, and that their salvation is intact.

I will admit, this element of REAPSOW will look different depending upon denominational adherences. But, as I've stated, a strategy is meant to be adaptable; it's not a model and we're not making crepes. However, I do believe that repentance, submission, and baptism should still be main factors, since the planter is not focused on transfer growth but conversion growth and reproducibility. Once the natural gospel conversations lead to salvation, baptism is tantamount with identity.

Much like Tertullian's early church catechumen apprenticeship-style of teaching and discipline, the planter assists in developing a new convert into a disciple of

Christ.[129] I view the equipping element (**E**) as probably one of the more neglected aspects of disciple-making. Recently, I was contracted to work with a major denomination to help assess their church planting efforts, build new structures, assessments, and curriculum, among other things. During my time, I continually observed that baptism was not something that generated the denomination's focus. Of course, since I was raised Episcopalian, moved to Methodist, married Presbyterian, dunked Pentecostal, educated in Southern Baptist seminaries, I understand denominational doctrines.

Nevertheless, Christian baptism "is an expression of solidarity with Jesus"[130] and, by instilling the importance of baptism's identity in Christ (Rom. 6:4) and the mission of God, the planter emphasizes their partaking in God's mission. In essence, the planter is equipping the new believer to become an essential part of the church's missional life. The unregenerate person is transformed into a redeemed sent-person, everywhere they go. Through baptism, all people are invited into the global mission of Christ's church.[131]

The purpose of the Great Commission focused on making disciples of Jesus by reproducing the Christ-life in new converts. As baptized followers of Christ, the disciples obediently obeyed Jesus as Lord (John 6:68). Jesus taught,

---

129 Tertullian, "Latin Christianity: Its Founder Tertullian." in vol. 3 *Ante-Nicene Fathers*, eds. Alexander Roberts and James Donaldson (Peabody: Hendrickson, 2004), 263.

130 John Nolland, *The Gospel of Matthew: A Commentary on the Greek Text.* (Grand Rapids: Carlisle, 2005), 1268.

131 Osborne, Grant R., *Matthew*, (Grand Rapids: Zondervan, 2010), 1080.

ate, and walked with the Twelve, intentionally expressing discipleship as a *way* of life. Jesus expected the disciples to make other sent-disciples.

Within the New Testament church, the new convert displayed faith in Christ's lordship through baptism, identifying a new life dedicated to the mission of God. Dorrow Maynard asserts that "Baptism thus impels us to mission."[132] As sent-out ones, believers become missional disciple-makers. A person cannot understand Christian baptism without highly regarding Christ's "missionary charge."[133] Baptism becomes the inaugurating, disciple-making component to which the new convert surrenders to "one Lord, one faith, one baptism" and to Christian spiritual formation within the church body (Eph. 4:1–6, 13–16).

In Acts, the repentance and submission of believing adults to acknowledge Christ as Lord occurred prior to baptism (Acts 2:38, 41, 8:36, 10:47). Therefore, baptism denoted a preceding submission to Christ conjoined by a discerning examination from another believer. As witnessed in the early church, before the new disciple became a part of the corporate body, new converts' baptism by immersion became mandatory.[134]

According to the Great Commission, during the baptism, the disciples would identify new believers with the "name" (*onoma*), of the "Father, Son, and Holy Spirit"

---

132 Maynard Dorrow, "Worship is Mission: Seeing the Eucharist as the Drama of God's Mission to the World," *Missio Apostolica* 9, no. 2 (2001): 78–83.

133 G. R. Beasley-Murray, *Baptism in the New Testament* (Eugene, OR: Wipf & Stock, 1972), 88.

134 Green, 218.

(Matt 28:19). Blomberg defines the usage of "the name" as "declaring allegiance to or becoming associated with the power and authority of Jesus."[135] The disciples are instructed to teach newly baptized believers to observe all that Jesus commanded.

Again, it needs to be reiterated, through baptism, all people are invited into the global mission of Christ's church.[136] No matter what denomination the planter resides, *Equipping as the Church* is an element not to be browsed over. Even though, throughout ecclesiology, the church did not retain a monolithic opinion regarding the *method* of baptism, biblically, baptism became the first obedient Christian action establishing a visible sign of repentance and the first step leading toward obedient discipleship.

Within the "ancient church," there was an existent "rule of faith."[137] Since most of the early church was illiterate, the rule of faith was memorized prior to baptism and then repeated upon the candidate partaking in the baptistic event. The Apostle's Creed, which would arrive a few centuries later, was derived from the early rule of faith being taught by the early church fathers—displaying the aspects of *Equipping as Church*.[138]

---

135 Craig Blomberg, *Matthew*, The New American Commentary (Nashville, TN: Broadman & Holman, 1992), 432.

136 Osborne, *Matthew*, 1080.

137 Benjamin K. Forrest, Joshua D. Chatraw, and Alister E. McGrath, eds. *The History of Apologetics: A Biographical and Methodological Introduction* (Grand Rapids: Zondervan, 2020), 93.

138 Ibid., 93.

Connecting the soul of the new disciple with the Godhead and within the obedient walk of the Christ-life is prayer. I would advise planters not to neglect or take for granted that everyone, or even anyone, understands prayer, how to do it, and why it's necessary. Even the disciples of Jesus asked Him how they were to pray (Luke 11:1). Prayer is more than a conversation with the Godhead (in which it is). Prayer is our connection and lifeline to mission.

As Philip Nation declares, "Prayer should bring about a sense of God's mission .... Prayer is not a separate spiritual discipline from God's mission. Prayer informs us of our role in His mission."[139] For this reason, making disciple-makers must include teaching and showing them how to pray, why to pray, and when to pray.

When I disciple a person, I first pray with them and for them. The next time we meet, I will begin with prayer and then after conversation, ask the person to finish with prayer. There is always a bit of trepidation that comes with learning to pray—especially in open spaces. I probably perform more than seventy-five percent of my disciple-making within busy coffee shops and public arenas. So, when I ask someone to pray, I am asking them to be bold in their faith, confident that God is listening, and to know that I am fully in agreement.

Because I am praying with them, I am displaying the applications of prayer, its importance, and the gravity of our mission. Over a short time period of time, I have watched

---

139 Nation, Philip, *Habits for Our Holiness: How the Spiritual Disciplines Grow Us Up, Draw Us Together, and Send Us Out* (Chicago: Moody, 2016), 79.

nervous, timid, and withdrawn people become emboldened "prayer-warriors," praying out loud for all to hear. This is why *Equipping as Church* is so important. We're teaching, training, and living life with one another and demonstrating the power of a collective body (in Christ). So, disciple-making is all about: you watch me do, we do together, I watch you, you show someone else, and so forth.

In essence, *Equipping as Church* is instructing new believers in all of the aspects of how and why the corporate body functions by utilizing life-on-life and communal praxis. The planter is leading and guiding a newly baptized convert into understanding and praying for the mission of the church (i.e. how does my life intersect with God's mission for the church?). The importance of godly leadership for apprenticeship cannot be stressed more. Nation suggests that, "The leadership that leads to holiness is what guides people toward God's redemptive work."[140] Therefore, disciple-making requires individual leadership (the planter) and also a communal collective (the church).

Disciple-making should always be viewed as reproducible, and prayer that solidifies and bolsters the mission of the church empowers a Christ-centered church. The planter has the ability to prepare new converts for gathering and scattering, as a measurable means of mission reproducibility.[141] But, by injecting missional prayer saturated DNA into a new convert about how the church functions, what the mission is all about, and with

---

140 Ibid., 185.

141 Hugh Halter and Matt Smay, *And: The Gathered and Scattered Church* (Grand Rapids: Zondervan, 2010), 125.

a beginning premise of reproducing self, the planter is assuring the collection of RDM believers.

Some of the successes that I've viewed during *Equipping as Church* are not only baptismal identity and bold-centered prayer warriors, but also in seeing a new convert being able to share their testimony and story with others. Ultimately, there is no greater feeling than to hear a salvation and transformation proclamation from a new disciple.

But again, disciple-making is not for the weak of heart, it takes time, investment, commitment, and dedication—disciples are not made overnight. As Alan Briggs affirms, "Cultivation of any kind will require four things: participation, partnership, patience, and produce."[142] However, a planter can expect participation when the starting DNA is about multiplicative reproducibility.

Assist through Mentorship

While some of the second century churches developed a three-year process for discipleship prior to baptism, instead of using time as a metric, RDM should be measured by life-on-life mentorship and mission.[143] The REAPSOW strategy exists as a deep discipleship process—and the majority of that process is relational mentoring on and for mission. Christian mentoring is a part of the disciple-making mission. As Ed Smither describes it, "Mentoring, in essence, means that a master, expert, or someone with

---

142 Briggs, Alan, *Staying Is the New Going: Choosing to Love Where God Places You* (Colorado Springs: NavPress, 2015), 34.

143 Green, 218.

significant experience is imparting knowledge and skill to a novice in an atmosphere of discipline, commitment, and accountability."[144] I may not be an expert, but I can impart the knowledge of what God has done in my life and how mission exists. I believe everyone ought to be discipling someone, and also be discipled (continually).

Alan Briggs sums up leadership training in this manner: "Formal learning is valuable, but apprenticeship is more balanced over the long haul."[145] Think of Paul and Silas, Paul and Timothy, or Paul and Barnabas, within each relationship dynamic a mentoring and mission aspect resided. Mentoring has always possessed an intrinsic "sentness." Whether the person was mentored in a trade, philosophy, or religion, the knowledge was meant to be used and applied to and for others. For Christianity, the development of disciple-makers has the sentness qualities and attributes of mission. Missional movements are empowered and enacted by devoted and dedicated Christ-followers.

As Hirsch rightly notes, "There is no other way to develop genuine transformational movements than through the critical task of disciple-making."[146] So, if disciple-making movements are the fulfillment of the Great Commission, then church planters ought to strive for reproducible mentorship (2 Tim. 2:2). While discipleship is

---

144 Smither, Ed, *Augustine as Mentor: A Model for Preparing Spiritual Leaders* (Nashville: B&H, 2008), 4.

145 Briggs, *Guardrails: Six Principles for a Multiplying Church* (Colorado Springs: NavPress, 2016), 57.

146 Hirsch, *Forgotten Ways*, 127.

the process, mentoring uses life-on-life actions (many of which are ethics-based), strategy, character issues, and trials.

Since life-on-life happens together amidst the daily rhythms, the mentor cannot hide emotions, decisions, and actions. Think about when the Apostle Paul was sentenced to jail in Philippi, Silas was also arrested (Acts 16:23–24). In prison, Paul mentors Silas by exuding his true character, humility, and patience, while also displaying strategy. Paul doesn't get upset, complain, or moan about being severely beaten, instead he's singing hymns and praising God (Acts 16:22–25). Paul also illustrates strategy as he doesn't pull out his Roman citizenship "card," but instead takes stripes for the Philippian church plant.

The whipping of Paul, an un-condemned Roman citizen, without a trial was punishable by death. Roman law was clear; every Roman citizen was to receive a trial prior to any punishment. By Paul not disclosing his citizenship card, as he does in other times (Acts 21:39, 22:25), he employs strategy. Once he reveals that he is a Roman citizen, he immediately quiets the Philippian magistrates—he has walking proof of their crime. The result? The Philippian church explodes! Without persecution or repercussion, the church grows exponentially and becomes the sole supporter of Paul's missional church planting journeys (Phil. 4:15–16).

What's the point? The point of illustrating Paul's imprisonment is that Silas was with Paul the entire time. Paul could not hide his emotions, even if he wanted to. True mentorship takes place where life happens, not solely in a classroom. As well, since discipleship is teaching people the actions, love, and life of Christ, mentorship conveys the "imitation" within disciple-making (2 Thess. 3:7–9; Heb. 13:7). As you may now be asking, is there a delineation between discipleship and mentorship? I'm sure some may see the use of semantics.

However, as I previously stated, discipleship and mentoring cannot be divorced, but I perceive that mentoring leads to more ethical, strategic, and life-on-life applied aspects of *how* to be a disciple-maker. As well, I would perceive discipleship to address the healthy habits and disciplines of the faith (prayer, fasting, obedience, worship, devotion). For instance, when Paul refused to take John Mark along on his second church planting journey (Acts 15:36–41), Paul was illustrating an ethical leadership decision based on Mark's character, experience, and practices. That was not a discipleship decision. Granted, it seemed to be the right choice, since Silas was imprisoned with Paul. Regardless, Silas would have received the message loud and clear, neglect of duty or failing to follow through on the mission is a serious charge. Paul was strategically mentoring Silas within the discipleship process.

And so, it seems that a planter should relationally engage in the life events of those he is discipling, as if an internship-style of life exists. If you're the mentor, allow your apprentice to see your hardships and trials and how you respond to them. Talk through them with him or her. With a firsthand account, they will see what living the Christ-life is all about.

Also, in the *Assist through Mentorship* stage (**A**), the planter is assessing each new believer in their personal character and motivation, along with their skills and abilities. As the church plant grows, the reality of mentoring each person is unlikely. I perceive that's why Jesus discipled the Twelve, but mentored the three (James, John, and Peter). Assisting in mentorship contains a reproducible DNA. The utilization of the question and answer method can be an edifying tool.

Questions are some of the best ways to mentor and coach people. Leadership should be about "how can I assist you to become better at what you're seeking." The church planter should be guiding his new disciples, letting out the leash, and allowing room for failure. Jesus continually allowed his disciples to make decisions—and sometimes they failed. If the disciples got it wrong, then Jesus addressed the issues by taking them aside. Jesus never ridiculed them out in the open. The Gospels consistently demonstrate Jesus as the mentor-questioner, expecting a response. Interaction and life-experiences are the best teachers. We learn more from our failures than our successes.

Questions for discipleship regard what is God doing, what is God saying, and how is God directing? While the questions of Christian mentoring relate to how do I *respond* to what God is doing, saying, and directing, remember, there is no mentorship if you're trying to do everything. You want people to do things for themselves. So, give them opportunities to serve and expect failures, mistakes, and learning experiences. Most of all, encourage them in working through the trials.

For the most part, it seems many lead planters want to do everything—as if one mistake ruins everything. But mentoring others allows for mistakes. Mistakes and failures become great learning opportunities. Life-on-life withness, intentionality, and invested time together, between the planter and disciple, are the focal point of the *Assist through Mentorship* phase.

Practice the Presence of Christ

Matthew's Great Commission passage is undoubtedly one of my favorites. But, academically, it has always brought about the discussion of the word "therefore." Whether we exegetically place "therefore" post or prior to the word, "go," the word *therefore* exists as a hinge—opening up the door to the reason how disciple-makers will be sent out on mission. Inevitably, they will be sent out with Christ-like authority.

For any disciple-maker, the Great Commission is a big fat sandwich. The words "go and make" is the meat of the sandwich—while Christ's authority (v18) and Christ's presence (v20) are the slices of bread. Connected to the Commission itself, Christ's disciple-making presence and resurrected authority are the assurity, hope, and peace provided to the disciples (Matt. 28:18–20). That's our peace, our authority, and our assurance is reaching, developing, and leading RDMs.

If there was ever a reason for the church planter to not fear and to be on mission with joy it is because the authority of Christ's presence is with him (Matt. 28:18, 20). Hence, the *Practice of Presence* component is an extension of the mentoring aspect, as the planter exhibits the lordship of Christ in the daily rhythms of life (home, recreational, bi-vocational work, ministerial). While the theological implication of the resurrection concerns the raising of the dead and the transformation of the corrupted believers' earthly bodies (Matt. 22:23–31; 1 Cor. 15:21), the missional mandate to the "end of the earth," assumes an accompanied power unlike any other!

Once a man of sorrow, acquainted with grief, stricken, smitten by God, and afflicted (Isa. 53:3–4), the resurrected Jesus arrived to stand before the disciples with the "supreme authority" of the universe.[147] The disciples first-hand witnessed that death had no authority over Jesus. This is good news to the planter.

This good news means that Jesus' authoritative language demanded a kingship response from everything in the existence of heaven, earth, and all of creation. I love R. C. H. Lenski's response to the Great Commission. He explains that Jesus rules over, "angels and archangels, powers, principalities, might, dominion, thrones, and the saints in glory ... over the evil spirit world, whose prince is conquered and despoiled, and whose hosts lie in abject submission beneath Jesus' feet."[148] The disciples had no need to worry about opposition with such a powerful commander in charge of the mission going with them— and neither should church planters, today.

I was once a hospice chaplain. During my first church plant, I served bi-vocationally. In actuality, I have worked bi-vocationally for over ten years. As a hospice chaplain there

---

147 Leon Morris, *The Gospel According to Matthew* (Grand Rapids: Eerdmans, 1992), 745–746.

148 R. C. H. Lenski, *The Interpretation of St. Matthew's Gospel* (Minneapolis: Augsburg Publishing House, 1961), 1171.

are certain parameters and guidelines that need to be met. The chaplain is present to provide spiritual care and dignity of life. Sometimes I did that through singing (perhaps my singing was a cause of death?), sometimes it was prayer, sometimes it was reading Scripture and devotionals, and other times it may have been with a conversation—if they were able. But, one thing we chaplains learned that was extremely important, we called it, the ministry of presence.

Sometimes the power of presence was/is stronger than words. For Alzheimer's and dementia patients, as well as those that did not feel up to a conversation, my very presence of being there—the spiritual care "expert," brought on a sense of peace and comfort to the afflicted. I didn't see myself as the expert, far from it, but for those that did, I saw an immediate sense of calm. Teaching disciples to practice the presence of Christ is similar.

Since the authority and presence of the Immanuel continually are with the planter, boldness becomes a church planter's quality (Matt. 1:23, 28:20). Boldness becomes an intrinsic attribute. The church planter ultimately engages in the application of resurrection power through courageous and bold risks for the kingdom (i.e. boldness of enduring trials via Christ's presence [Phil. 3:10]). In these risk-taking bold actions, the planter is showing the apprentice how to navigate troubled waters. Church planting has always been risky, bold and lonely, but the presence of the King brings constant calm.

I believe a church planter has a high risk in their workload, sometimes creating a necessity to trust Christ and His presence of peace (Eph. 2:14). In making disciple-makers, the aspects of Christ's peace, boldness, and presence are essential because the overall goal of disciple-making is reproducibility and mission. Navigating and understanding the trials of church planting and the coinciding risks become a vital aspect to overcome. In like manner, the new disciple is probably facing some of the same types of challenges, risks of their own, and trials.

Maybe some of the friends of the new disciple have left them. Perhaps, the new disciple is feeling lonely and depressed. These two areas of loneliness and depression seem to be regular baggage for church planting pioneers. Teaching disciples to trust in Christ *because* He has ultimate authority and is always with us is imperative. Essentially, what the planter desires to see from his apprentice is the presence, boldness, and peace of Christ.

Spirit Empowerment

From my research in Acts 1:8, which happens to be one of the favorite passages of my church planting partner, Jonathan Collier, Jesus stated that the Holy Spirit leads, guides, and enables the disciple-maker for missional engagement.[149] Frequently, Jonathan and I have great discussions about Acts 1:8—the reality of how the disciples stood gazing up into the heavens afterwards (vertical blindness)—assuredly, an awkward moment for all. We also talk about how misconstrued the power of the Spirit is utilized or presented today, or in some cases, completely neglected.

---

149 Millard J. Erickson, *Christian Theology* (Grand Rapids, MI: Baker Books, 2009), 889.

Jesus explained the power of the Holy Spirit was something for the disciples to receive—but that was pre-Pentecost. We receive the Spirit of God upon conversion. However, I think an applicable connection to Acts 1:8 is understanding the Spirit's role in the mission of God.

Just as the Spirit guided Israel with a cloud by day and fire by night, He, too, will guide the church on its mission. This *Spirit Empowerment (S)* section launches the second phase of the REAPSOW strategy. If all we did was reap, we would eventually have no fruit, no growth, and plants would wither away with no replenishment or vitality.

So, the SOW phase of the training shifts from solely the planter discipling and mentoring the new disciple, to the planter continuing that process while overseeing the apprentice beginning to disciple someone new. In the first aspect of the SOW phase, *Spirit Empowerment* is necessary. Holy Spirit empowerment is essential to all believers, then again, all believers should be acting as disciple-makers. But, one of the ways that Holy Spirit empowerment is evidenced is by fruit (Gal. 5:22–23).

As Jesus told the disciples to wait until they were "clothed with power from on high" (Luke 24:49), the planter emphasizes that the Holy Spirit is the enabling power given to all the newly gathered saints. During this phase, the planter should visibly be witnessing his disciple walking through life, discipling another person. While the apprentice begins working with someone else at the REAP stage of the practicum, the planter is guiding that disciple through the SOW phase with Spirit awareness, boldness, peace, power, and direction.

The *Spirit Empowerment* element focuses on the disciplines of prayer walking, understanding Scripture, collective prayer, and discernment from the Spirit of God. Are you hearing from God? What is God speaking to you? Those are some good applicable questions.

The planter must cultivate and demonstrate the hearing and perceiving of the Holy Spirit's voice. In addition, the planter guides the disciple in seeking the Spirit's guidance for evangelism, expounding and teaching the Scriptures, leading and guiding a group of believers, and building a culture of discipleship with newly gathered believers. This is when the planter should begin to notice the formulation of a church body. People are being invited and you're connecting them with disciples to be discipled.

The planter should guide the disciple through noted journaling about specific Holy Spirit led events, situations, and circumstances in order to instruct in Holy Spirit awareness and listening. Journaling provides the planter the opportunity to celebrate the Holy Spirit moments within the disciple's life and ministry.

By this phase of the REAPSOW, the planter should witness the disciple beginning the early stages of developing into a leader/mentor. The trained apprentice should be able to have natural gospel conversations, gather one or more converts into a small group and build a culture of discipleship. At this stage, the church plant development has entered the famous incubator stage—you're essentially growing by RDM.

During the incubator stage, the church planter should be witnessing real fruit and reproducibility—the invested time of the REAP phase is now paying "dividends." A focused time of listening to the Holy Spirit's guiding and leading effectively assists in the development of vision and mission for the new church plant to bless and reach the community.

Obedience-based Discipleship

Creating an element of reproducible disciple-making labeled *Obedience-based Discipleship* (O) may seem redundant, but making disciple-makers isn't merely following Jesus;

it requires submission to Christ. I like to say it this way, when I was at the age of eleven, I gave my life to Christ, but I didn't submit to Christ until I was thirty. There's a big difference in giving and submitting. At the heart of the Great Commission are the commands for new disciples to "observe all" that Christ commanded (Matt. 28:18–20). Clearly, the disciples had observed all of the everyday actions, emotions, and practices of Jesus.

Furthermore, there's no existing chasm between Jesus' life and the examples of disciple-making.[150] Jesus demonstrated what an obedient life looked like and how to make disciple-makers while living out that life. For example, in the Garden of Gethsemane, Jesus obediently followed the Father's plan and direction, laying aside his own will, for God's (Matt. 26:39). In like manner, obediently following

---

150 David L. Turner, *Matthew*, ECNT (Grand Rapids: Baker Academic, 2008), 957.

the commands of Christ denotes responding to the loving commands of Christ and his teachings (John 14:15).[151]

Jesus declared a cost of discipleship (Luke 14:25–33). The O strategy element utilizes combined didactic and practical training. I'm of the belief that the obedience command is directly related to the love command of Christ. Jesus declared, "A new commandment I give to you, that you love one another: just as I have loved you, you also are to love one another. By this all people will know that you are my disciples, if you have love for one another." (John 13:34–35). It becomes apparent that the world will know Christians are disciples of Jesus by their love for one another—something most believers seem to neglect.

Church planters learn to live out the love commands of Christ in and through daily life (Matt. 28:19–20). A person cannot be a church planter and dislike people, although I have seen it. For the Apostle Paul wrote, "For the love of Christ controls us" (2 Cor. 5:14). Therefore, teaching is more than head knowledge of what Jesus declared, but by the very action of self-sacrifice and humility, as the bodily Godhead, Jesus demonstrated an amazing and great love —an unconditional love. In turn, disciples of His are to "obey" the love commands of Christ.

One way that disciple-makers illustrate their love for one another is in communally gathering together for the teaching of the Scriptures, fellowship, and the breaking of bread (Acts 2:42–47). Obedient discipleship exists only

---

151 R. T. France, *The Gospel of Matthew*, TNIC (Grand Rapids: Eerdmans, 2007), 1119.

with intentionality. During the *Obedience* phase, the newly forming church participates in life together as a missional ecclesiastical community.

The church planter can teach others, with the apprentice, in obediently following Christ—by taking the role of serving, leading, instructing, and "carrying out" the commands of Jesus to live the Christ-life (1 John 5:2). Patience and love toward others, holiness to God, compassion for the outcast, and a dedicated heart for the lost, compose the focus of the *Obedience-based Discipleship* phase.

Witness by Withness

Choosing one of the seven elements as more instrumental to spiritual growth and reproducibility over another would be quite difficult, but by far one of my favorites is this one. The *Witness by Withness (W)* rounds out the REAPSOW strategy. The mission of God, *missio Dei*, not only brings church planters into unknown, unfamiliar, unsaved, and unengaged areas of the world (four "uns"), but also of those same dynamics within a home community.

Similar to the "withness" created between Jesus and the disciples, missional relationships develop by investing in the welfare of others.[152] The *missio Dei* is an "incarnational movement of the Son, in its historical and eschatological movement through his people, by the Spirit."[153] While that last sentence may have sounded really theological, its basic meaning is that the story of God is a meta-narrative. The

---

152 Reid and Robinson, *With*, 16.

153 Hastings, *Missional God, Missional Church*, 91.

Bible is not composed of unconnected short stories about how to be a better person, what not to do, to do, or how to live an ethical or moral life. The Bible also isn't about religion. The Bible is the story of God and His creation (Luke 24:27, 44; John 1:1, Rev. 19:13). Of course, the Bible is more in-depth of the aforementioned, but it is a meta-narrative about history and future and where they collide.

The church fulfills the mission of God by incarnating as the body of Christ within communities everywhere. Consequently, there is no coincidence that REAPSOW's last element has to do living a life of withness on mission. The mission is everywhere; remember, we're church planters, we're supposed to be surrounded.

However, do not misconstrue this strategy. REAPSOW was never meant to be completed, only continually duplicated over and over again. REAPSOW is about multiplicative reproducibility—in essence, multiplying disciple-making people. We ought also note that the biblical word for discipleship denotes three areas of development: deliverance from sin, development as an obedient follower of Jesus, and deployment into the world to proclaim Jesus Christ as Lord.[154]

Acts 1:8 commissions believers to become Christ's "witnesses." Just as Christ sent out the disciples two-by-two (Luke 10:1), during the last cyclical phase of REAPSOW, the planter is creating an *ethos* of "withness"—as the body of Christ proclaims the gospel of Christ, together, to others. At this point, I'm obviously assuming that the planter has utilized an Anchor Trade, discovered the Mars Hill, began

---

154 Hull, *The Complete Book of Discipleship*, 34.

inculturating others with natural gospel conversations, and has developed more than one RDM apprentice who, in turn, is discipling other disciple-makers.

From a larger scale, the REAPSOW training strategy focuses on the planter reproducing a biblical mindset of collective missional witness to "Jerusalem, Judea, Samaria, and to the end of the world" (Acts 1:8).[155] A core group of committed believers should be effectively participating and engaging in the mission of God, together. Withness in Christian love is a powerful witness.

The praxis of *Witness by Withness* exists through natural conversation, relationship building, and evangelistic principles, namely, the reproducing of phase one—*Reaching New Converts (R)*. This entire strategy is meant to be cyclical. The core group should be engaging in both gathering and scattering together as a unified church body.

Conclusion

I should stress as I began, REAPSOW is *not* a red bat. There is no red bat! What REAPSOW should be to you is an adaptable strategy, as it is to me. I utilize this strategy in practical ways to remind myself of being an obedient disciple-maker. Am I living my life according the biblical concepts presented by Jesus? Are certain areas stronger in my life than others? If so, what are the weaker areas of my disciple-making? Can I look back and see multiplication

---

155 George Robinson, *Striking the Match: How God Is Using Ordinary People to Change the World Through Short- Term Missions* (Franklin, TN: E3 Resources, 2008), 171.

in my life (generations of disciples)? Are the people that I've discipled been on mission? Did I go with them as a mentor? Is my life transparent to those living the Christ-life with me?

The fact of the matter is that we're all students of the Scriptures. We should be learning from one another (Prov. 27:17). You, like me, should be able to glean what is applicable, teachable, and practical within all of our resources, to better help us better reach our four "uns". I've always admitted, if a strategy is not adaptable, then it is a model, not a strategy.

Strategies are adjustable. Anyone who has ever planted a church understands the great need for adaptability. Culture changes rapidly. Yet, I truly believe that if I adhere to the principles of *Reaching New Converts, Equipping as Church, Assisting by Mentoring, Practice the Presence of Christ, Spirit Empowerment, Obedience Based Discipleship,* and *Witness by Witness* that I will be making disciple-makers that make disciple-makers, creating missional movements, and establishing missional churches.

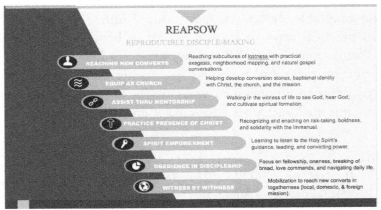

Bibliography

Allen, Rolland. *The Spontaneous Expansion of the Church*. Eugene: Wipf and Stock. 1962.

Balzer, Tracy. *Thin Places: An Evangelical Journey into Celtic Christianity*. Abilene: Leafwood. 2007.

Barna, George and David Kinnaman. *Churchless: Understanding Today's Unchurched and How to Connect with Them*. Carol Stream, IL: Tyndale House Publishers. 2014.

Beasley-Murray, G. R. *Baptism in the New Testament*. Eugene, OR: Wipf & Stock, 1972.

Blomberg, Craig. *Matthew*. The New American Commentary. Nashville, TN: Broadman & Holman. 1992.

Bonem, Mike. *In Pursuit of Great and Godly leadership: Tapping the Wisdom of the World for the Kingdom of God*. San Francisco: Jossey-Bass. 2012.

Boren, M. Scott. *Missional Small Groups: Becoming a Community That Makes a Difference in the World*. Grand Rapids, MI: Baker Books. 2010.

Bosch, David, J. *Transforming Mission: Paradigm Shifts in theology of Mission*. Maryknoll: Orbis. 2009.

Breen, Mike. *Leading Missional Communities: Rediscovering the Power of Living on Mission Together.* Pawleys Island, SC: 3DM. 2013.

Briggs, Alan. *Guardrails: Six Principles for a Multiplying Church.* Colorado Springs: NavPress. 2016.

————. *Staying Is the New Going: Choosing to Love Where God Places You.* Colorado Springs: NavPress. 2015.

Calvin, John. *Calvin's Commentaries.* XVII, trans. William Pringle. Grand Rapids, MI: Baker Academic, 2005, 385.; John Calvin c. 1509–1564.

Coy, Terry. *Facing the Change: Challenges and Opportunities for an American Missiology.* Oklahoma: Tate. 2013.

Dodds, Adam. "Newbigin's Trinitarian missiology: the doctrine of the Trinity as good news for Western culture." *International Review of Mission* 99, no. 390 (April 1, 2010): 17. *ATLA Religion Database with ATLASerials,* EBSCO*host.* accessed July 6, 2015.

Dorrow, Maynard. "Worship is Mission: Seeing the Eucharist as the Drama of God's Mission to the World." *Missio Apostolica 9.* no. 2. 2001.

Erickson, Millard J. *Christian Theology.* Grand Rapids, MI: Baker Books. 2009.

Forrest, Benjamin K., Joshua D. Chatraw, and Alister E. McGrath, eds. *The History of Apologetics: A Biographical and Methodological Introduction.* Grand Rapids: Zondervan. 2020.

France, R. T. *The Gospel of Matthew*, TNIC. Grand Rapids, MI: Eerdmans, 2007.

Gallaty, Robby. *Growing Up: How to Be a Disciple Who Makes Disciples.* Bloomington, IN: Crossbooks. 2013.

Garrison, David. *Church Planting Movements: How God is Redeeming a Lost World.* ArkeDelphia: WIGTake. 2004.

Goheen, Michael. *The Church and Its Vocation: Lesslie Newbigin's Missionary Ecclesiology.* Grand Rapids: Baker. 2018.

Gray, Derwin, L. *The High Definition Leader: Building Multiethnic Churches in a Multiethnic World.* Nashville: Thomas Nelson. 2015.

Greear, J. D. *Gaining by Losing: Why the Future Belongs to Churches that Send.* Grand Rapids, MI: Zondervan.2015.

Green, Michael. *Evangelism in the Early Church.* Grand Rapids, MI: Eerdmans. 2003.

Halter, Hugh, and Matt Smay. *And: The Gathered and Scattered Church.* Grand Rapids: Zondervan. 2010.

Harvey, Charles Edward. 1982. "John D Rockefeller, Jr and the Interchurch World Movement of 1919-1920: a different angle of the ecumenical movement." *Church History* 51, no. 2: 203. *ATLA Religion Database with ATLASerials*, EBSCO*host*. accessed July 7, 2015.

Hastings, Ross. *Missional God, Missional Church: Hope for Re-Evangelizing the West.* Downers Grove: InterVarsity Press. 2012.

Hemphill, Ken. *Revitalizing the Sunday Morning Dinosaur: A Sunday School Growth Strategy for the 21st Century.* Nashville, TN: Broadman & Holman. 1996.

Henrichsen, Walter A. *Disciples Are Made, Not Born: Helping Others Grow to Maturity in Christ.* Colorado Springs, CO: David C. Cook. 1988.

Hesselgrave, David J. *Planting Churches Cross-Culturally: North America and Beyond.* Grand Rapids, MI: Baker Academic. 2008.

Hirsch, Alan. *The Forgotten Ways: Reactivating Apostolic Movements.* Grand Rapids: Brazos. 2016.

————. and Dave Ferguson. *On the Verge: A Journey into the Apostolic Future of the Church.* Grand Rapids, MI: Zondervan. 2011.

————. *Reactivating the Missional Church: The Forgotten Ways: Reactivating the Missional Church.* Grand Rapids: Baker. 2006.

Hull, Bill. *Conversion & Discipleship.* Grand Rapids, MI: Zondervan. 2016.

————. *The Complete Book of Discipleship: On Being and Making Followers of Christ.* Colorado Springs, CO: NavPress. 2006.

Kittel, Gerhard, Geoffrey W. Bromiley, and Gerhard Friedrich, eds., *Theological Dictionary of the New Testament.* Grand Rapids, MI: Eerdmans. 1964.

Lenski, R. C. H. *The Interpretation of St. Matthew's Gospel.* Minneapolis, MN: Augsburg Publishing House. 1961.

Little, Franklin H. *The Origins of Sectarian Protestantism.* New York, NY: Beacons. 1964.

Logan, Bob. *The Church Planting Journey.* 2019.

Malphurs, Aubrey. *Look Before You Lead: How to Discern and Shape Your Church Culture.* Grand Rapids, MI: Baker Books. 2013.

———. *Planting Growing Churches For the 21ˢᵗ Century: A Comprehensive Guide for New Churches and Those Desiring Renewal.* 3ʳᵈ Ed. Grand Rapids, MI: Baker Books. 2004.

McGowan, Andrew B. *Ancient Christian Worship: Early Church Practices in Social, Historical, and Theological Perspective.* Grand Rapids, MI: Baker Academic. 2014.

McManus, Erwin Raphael. *An Unstoppable Force Daring to Become the Church God Had in Mind 2001 Publication.* Loveland, CO: Group Pub. Inc. 2000.

Moore, Ralph. *Making Disciples: Developing Lifelong Followers of Jesus Christ.* Ventura, CA: Regal. 2012.

Morris, Leon. *The Gospel According to Matthew.* Grand Rapids: Eerdmans. 1992.

Nation, Philip. *Habits for Our Holiness: How the Spiritual Disciplines Grow Us Up, Draw Us Together, and Send Us Out.* Chicago: Moody. 2016.

Newbigin, Lesslie. *Foolishness to the Greeks: The Gospel and Western Culture.* Grand Rapids, MI: Wm. B. Eerdmans Publishing Co. 1988.

————. *The Other Side of 1984: Questions for the Churches.* Geneva: World Council of Churches. 1983.

Nolland, John. *The Gospel of Matthew: A Commentary on the Greek Text.* Grand Rapids, MI: Carlisle. 2005.

Ogden, Greg. *Transforming Discipleship: Making Disciples a Few at a Time.* Downers Grove, IL: InterVarsity Press. 2003.

Olson, David T. *The American Church in Crisis: Groundbreaking Research Based on a National Database of Over 200,000 Churches.* Grand Rapids, MI: Zondervan. 2008.

Osborne, Grant R. *Matthew.* Grand Rapids, MI: Zondervan. 2010.

————. "Moving Forward on Our Knees: Corporate Prayer in the New Testament." *Journal of the Evangelical Theological Society.* 53, no. 2 June 2010.

Ott, Craig, and Gene Wilson. *Global Church Planting: Biblical Principles and Best Practices for Multiplication.* Grand Rapids, MI: Baker Academic. 2011.

Payne, J.D. *Pressure Points: Twelve Global Issues Shaping the Face of the Church.* Nashville, TN: Thomas Nelson. 2013.

Putman, Jim and Bobby Harrington. *Discipleshift: Five Steps to Make Disciples Who Make Disciples.* Grand Rapids, MI: Zondervan. 2013.

Reid, Alvin R., and George G. Robinson. *With: A Practical Guide to Informal Mentoring and Intentional Disciple Making.* Lexington, KY: Rainer Publishing, 2016.

Riel, Jennifer, and Roger L. Martin. *Creating Great Choices: A leader's Guide to Integrative Thinking.* Boston: Harvard Business Review. 2017.

Robinson, George. *Striking the Match: How God is Using Ordinary People to Change the World Through Short-Term Missions.* Franklin, TN: E3 Resources. 2008.

Rudy-Froese, Allan. "Learning from Luther on Christian discipleship." *Vision. Winnipeg, Man.* 13, no. 2 (September 2012): 55–63.; Reformation period (c. 1517–1648), Martin Luther c. 1483–1546.

Schaff, Philip, and David Schley Schaff, *History of the Christian Church.* Vol 2. (Grand Rapids: C. Scribner. 1910.

Schnabel, Eckhard J. *Early Christian Mission,* vol. 1 & 2. Downers Grove, IL: InterVarsity Press. 2004.

Schreiner, Thomas R., and Shawn Wright, eds. *Believer's Baptism: Sign of the New Covenant in Christ.* Nashville, TN: Broadman & Holman, 2007.

Smither, Ed. *Augustine as Mentor: A Model for Preparing Spiritual Leaders.* Nashville: B & H. 2008.

———. "Learning from Patristic Evangelism and Discipleship,"

———. *The Contemporary Church and the Early Church.* Eugene: Wipf & Stock. 2010.

Stetzer, Ed. *Planting Missional Churches.* Nashville, TN: Broadman & Holman Publishers. 2006.

Surratt, Chris. *Small Groups for the Rest of Us: How to Design Your Small-Groups System to Reach the Ages.* Nashville, TN: Thomas Nelson. 2015.

Turner, David L. *Matthew,* ECNT. Grand Rapids, MI: Baker Academic. 2008.

Tertullian. "Latin Christianity: its Founder Tertullian." in vol. 3 *Ante-Nicene Fathers,* eds. Alexander Roberts and James Donaldson. Peabody, MA: Hendrickson. 2004.

Turnau, Ted. *Popologetics: Popular Culture in Christian Perspective.* Phillipsburg, NJ: P & R Publishing. 2012.

Vanhoozer, Kevin J., Charles A. Anderson, and Michael J. Sleasman, eds. *Everyday Theology: How to Read Cultural Texts and Interpret Trends.* Grand Rapids, MI: Baker Academic. 2007.

Verduin, Leonard. *The Reformers and Their Stepchildren. (Dissent and Nonconformity)* Paris: The Baptist Standard Bearer. 2001.

Wagner, Peter, C. *Strategies for Church Growth: Tools for Effective Mission and Evangelism.* Ventura, CA: Regal Books. 1987.

Walton, Steve. "What Does 'Mission' in Acts Mean in Relation to the 'Powers That Be'?" *Journal of the Evangelical Theological Society.* 55, no. 3 2012.

Webber, Robert. *Ancient-Future Faith: Rethinking Evangelicalism for a Postmodern World.* Grand Rapids, MI: Baker Academic, 1999.

Woodward, JR. *Creating a Missional Culture: Equipping the Church for the Sake of the World.* Downers Grove, IL: IVP Books. 2012.

Wright, N.T., and Michael F. Bird. *The New Testament in Its World: An Introduction to the History, Literature, and Theology of the First Christians.* Grand Rapids: Zondervan. 2019.

Made in the USA
Monee, IL
26 September 2020